Jams, Jellies, Pickles & Chutneys

G000042293

Jams, Jellies, Pickles & Chutneys

Mary Norwak

Bounty Books

First published in Great Britain in 1985 by
Ward Lock Limited, a division of Octopus Publishing Group Ltd

This edition published in 2011 by Bounty Books,
a division of Octopus Publishing Group Ltd,
Endeavour House
189 Shaftesbury Avenue
London WC2H 8JY
www.octopusbooks.co.uk

An Hachette UK Company
www.hachette.co.uk

Copyright © Mary Norwak 1985

All rights reserved. No part of this work may be reproduced or utilized in
any form or by any means, electronic or mechanical, including photocopying,
recording or by any information storage and retrieval system, without the
prior written permission of the publisher

ISBN: 978-0-753721-92-6

A CIP catalogue record for this book is available from the British Library

Printed and bound in China

CONTENTS

Acknowledgements
Cover photograph by Eric Carter

Photography on pages 17, 21, 25, 37, 41, 49, 57, 69 and 77 by Peter Myers
Home Economist   Clare Gordon-Smith
Stylist   Alison Williams

Illustrations by Dick Vine

Photographs on pages 29, 45 and 65 supplied courtesy of The Citrus Marketing Board of Israel, The Fresh Fruit and Vegetable Information Bureau **and** Tate and Lyle Refineries respectively.

The author and publisher would like to thank the following companies for sponsoring photographs:
Sarsons Malt Vinegars (page 57) **and** Silver Spoon Sugars (pages 21 and 37)
and
David Mellor for loaning the preserving pan on page 37.

Sugar for photography provided by The Silver Spoon Creative Kitchen.

Notes
It is important to follow the metric, imperial *or* the American measures when using the recipes in this book. Do not use a combination of measures.

American terminology is indicated by the use of brackets both in the list of ingredients and in the methods.

American measures which follow metric and imperial measures within the recipe methods are preceded by the term 'US'.

Introduction

Once upon a time, most houses had their stillroom and larder. The mistress of the house was in charge of the preserving of food, and, with the help of her servants, would be responsible for drying herbs, fruit and vegetables; candying and crystallizing fruit and flowers; potting jams and preparing pickles, chutneys and sauces; making wines, cordials and liqueurs; and salting or potting meat. A country household was totally self-sufficient, but preserving was necessary to ensure food supplies right through the year, when animals might have to be killed because of lack of fodder and every scrap of food was precious.

As commercial food processing became more sophisticated, the need for preserving food at home became less essential. Additionally, the development of the home freezer has created an easy and quick way of preserving. Nevertheless, there is a continued interest in making sweet and sour preserves for use as accompaniments, toppings, fillings, and, generally, to give variety to meals.

Glut fruit and vegetables can be made into all kinds of preserves. Equipment is very simple, and preparation is easy once the basic principles are understood.

My particular thanks are due to the staff of the Home Food Storage and Preservation Section of Long Ashton Research Station, Bristol, whose work in the field of home preserving is invaluable.

Mary Norwak

JAMS

There is an endless variety of jams to be made, particularly if fruits are combined. This means that some common fruit such as apples and rhubarb can be used as bulk ingredients combined with a more special fruit such as raspberries to give more interesting jams in larger quantities.

Equipment

Use a large preserving pan in which preserves can be boiled rapidly without boiling over. The pan should be wide to allow rapid evaporation of liquid which is essential to good setting. Use an aluminium, stainless steel or copper pan (chipped enamel is dangerous, while zinc or iron spoil colour and flavour). Copper will keep green fruits green, but can spoil the colour of red fruit.

Additional useful items are a metal or heatproof glass jug for pouring jam into jars cleanly and easily; a slotted metal spoon for skimming jams; a long-handled wooden spoon which prevents hot jam splashing on the hands, and accurate scales or, for Americans, measuring cups. A sugar thermometer takes the guesswork out of jam-making as it records the temperature at which preserves set; it is, however, not essential, and the setting tests on page 9 are quite adequate.

Jam jars may be saved from year to year, and screw-top honey jars, coffee jars and preserving jars are very useful.

Waxed paper discs, transparent covers and labels can be bought in packets, or tight-fitting plastic covers can be used.

Ingredients

FRUIT

Fresh, sound fruit that is not wet or mushy should be used. It should be slightly under-ripe, as very ripe fruit has a reduced pectin and sugar content and will affect the setting and keeping quality of preserves.

ACID

Acid is added to some fruit during cooking to extract pectin, improve colour and prevent crystallization – it should be added to any fruit with a low acid content, and to any vegetable jam. Acid may be in the form of lemon juice, citric or tartaric acid powder, redcurrant or gooseberry juice. To 2kg/4 lb fruit, allow $2 \times 15ml$ spoons/2 tablespoons lemon juice or $1 \times 2.5ml$ spoon/½ teaspoon citric acid powder or 125ml/¼ pint/1¼ US cups redcurrant or gooseberry juice.

PECTIN

The setting quality of jam depends on its pectin content, and some types of fruit have a higher pectin content than others, so that they are good 'mixers' with other fruits. Cooking apples, blackcurrants, damsons, gooseberries, plums, quinces and redcurrants are all high in pectin, and preserves made with them always set well. Fresh apricots, early blackberries, greengages and loganberries have a lower pectin content.

Fruit and vegetables which are low in pectin include late blackberries, cherries, elderberries, marrows, medlars, pears, rhubarb, strawberries and tomatoes, and these generally need mixing with high-pectin fruit, or juice made from such fruit, while acid will help to release the pectin.

SUGAR

Preserving sugar is ideal for jam-making, but is expensive and not always easy to obtain. Cube or granulated sugar is perfectly satisfactory. Sugar must be stirred carefully into the cooked fruit until dissolved, then the liquid boiled rapidly so that crystals do not remain and burn on the bottom of the pan.

Sugar may be warmed slightly in the oven before being added to the fruit; this speeds up the dissolving process.

Basic Method

Assemble all equipment and ingredients before cooking, and follow recipes carefully for perfect results.

Wash and drain fruit, and remove stems, leaves and bruised or damaged pieces. Some fruit may be cooked whole and the stones removed during cooking, or the stones may be removed beforehand. Apricot, cherry, plum and greengage jams can be flavoured with a few kernels from their stones. The fruit should be cooked slowly in water until completely tender, adding acid during this cooking if specified. When the fruit is soft and the contents of the pan reduced by about one-half, the sugar should be stirred in over low heat until dissolved. After that, the jam must be boiled rapidly, without stirring, to setting point (see below), and should be tested after 5 minutes. Some jams take longer, but no jam needs to boil longer than 20 minutes. After testing for setting, skim the jam and leave it to cool for a minute or two before stirring so that the fruit does not rise in the jars.

Pour the jam into hot, clean jars, filling right to the brim, and put on waxed paper discs at once, pressing carefully to exclude air bubbles. Put on top covers and clean the jars, then label and store in a cool, dry place.

SETTING TESTS

A well-keeping jam should have 60% added sugar content or three parts sugar to five parts fruit. When the jam reaches setting point, remove it from the heat at once.

Temperature test. Place a sugar thermometer in hot water. Stir the jam and submerge the thermometer bulb completely in the jam. When it registers 104°C/220°–221°F, the jam is cooked.

Weight test. Weigh the pan and spoon before cooking begins. When the jam weighs 5kg/10 lb for every 3kg/6 lb/12 us cups of sugar used, the jam is ready. To work out the final correct weight, multiply the quantity of sugar used by ten and divide by six.

Flake test. Dip a clean wooden spoon in the boiling jam. Let the cooling jam drop from the spoon, and if the drops run together and form a flake, the jam is ready.

Plate test. Put a little jam on an old plate or saucer, and leave it to become cold. If the jam forms a skin and wrinkles when pushed with a spoon or finger, it is ready. The preserving pan should be taken off the heat while the test jam is cooling.

Preserving Faults

Mouldy jam – results from damp fruit, insufficient boiling, poor storage, badly filled or covered jars.

Crystallized jam – indicates too much sugar in proportion to fruit or over-cooking jam to stiffen it when too little sugar has been used. Over-cooking and poor stirring, resulting in undissolved sugar, can also cause the problem.

Fermenting, 'winey' jam – results from over-ripe fruit, insufficient sugar or boiling, poor covering and bad storage.

Hard dry jam – results from over-boiling or bad covering when jam is stored in a warm place. Plastic or screw-tops will help to prevent this problem.

Syrupy jam – results from lack of pectin, insufficient boiling or over-boiling past setting point.

Poor flavour – results from over- or under-ripe fruit, too much sugar, too slow boiling or over-boiling.

Poor colour – results from poor quality fruit, a poor quality preserving pan or from storing in a bright light. It can also arise if the fruit is not cooked slowly enough to soften it completely, if the jam is over-boiled or boiled too slowly to setting point.

APPLE JAM

Metric/imperial		American
1.5kg/3 lb	cooking apples	3 lb
500ml/1 pint	water	2½ cups
2 × 5ml spoons/ 2 teaspoons	citric acid powder	2 teaspoons
	6 cloves	
	sugar	

Cut the apples into slices without peeling or coring. Put them into the pan with the water, acid and cloves, and simmer until very soft.

Remove the cloves and sieve the apples. Weigh the sieved pulp and allow 375g/12 oz/¾ US cup sugar to each 500g/1 lb/ 1 US cup pulp.

Return the apple pulp to the pan, add the sugar, and stir over low heat until it is dissolved, then boil rapidly to setting point. Skim the jam, pour into hot jars, then cover and label.

APPLE GINGER JAM

Metric/imperial		American
1.5kg/3 lb	cooking apples	3 lb
500ml/1 pint	water	2½ cups
1 × 5ml spoon/ 1 teaspoon	ground ginger	1 teaspoon
	2 lemons	
1.5kg/3 lb	sugar	6 cups
100g/4 oz	crystallized ginger, chopped	½ cup

Peel and core the apples, and put the peel and cores into a piece of muslin. Tie the muslin into a bag shape and put it into a pan. Cut the apples into pieces and put them into the pan with the water, ground ginger, grated lemon peel (rind) and their juice. Simmer the mixture over low heat until the fruit is soft.

Take out the bag of peel and cores, and squeeze the juice from the bag into the apples. Stir in the sugar and chopped ginger over low heat until the sugar has dissolved. Boil the mixture rapidly until it reaches setting point, then skim, pour into hot jars, cover and label.

Autumn Jam

Metric/imperial		American
1 kg/2 lb	cooking apples	2 lb
1 kg/2 lb	ripe pears	2 lb
1 kg/2 lb	plums	2 lb
25g/1 oz	root (fresh) ginger, unpeeled and roughly chopped	scant ¼ cup
2.5kg/5 lb	sugar	10 cups

Peel and core the apples and pears, and put them into a pan. Skin the plums, cut them in half and remove the stones. Add them to the other fruit in the pan. Put the ginger into a piece of muslin, and tie it into a bag, then put the bag into the pan.

Simmer the fruit gently over low heat until the fruit is soft but not broken, adding a little water if necessary to prevent burning, though the fruit should yield plenty of juice.

Stir in the sugar over low heat until it is dissolved, then boil the mixture rapidly to setting point. Skim, then pour the jam into hot jars, cover and label.

Blackberry and Rhubarb Jam

Metric/imperial		American
2kg/4 lb	blackberries	4 lb
375ml/¾ pint	water	2 cups
1 kg/2 lb	rhubarb	2 lb
	sugar	

Wash the berries and remove any stems and unripe berries. Simmer them in the water until tender, then sieve them to remove all the seeds.

Wash and chop the rhubarb, then put it into a pan with the berry pulp. Simmer the mixture until the rhubarb is soft.

Weigh the fruit mixture and allow 500g/1 lb/1 us cup sugar to each 500g/1 lb/1 us cup fruit.

Return the fruit mixture to the pan, and stir in the sugar over low heat until dissolved, then boil rapidly to setting point. Skim, then pour the jam into hot jars, cover and label.

Note This is a good jam to make from the last of the rhubarb crop which will be finishing when the blackberries come into season.

BLACKBERRY AND APPLE JAM

Metric/imperial		American
2kg/4 lb	blackberries	4 lb
250ml/½ pint	water	1¼ cups
1kg/2 lb	cooking apples	2 lb
3kg/6 lb	sugar	12 cups

Wash the blackberries and remove any stems and unripe berries. Put the berries into a pan with half the water, and simmer until tender.

Peel, core and slice the apples. Simmer them gently in the remaining water until they are soft but are not breaking up.

Combine the two fruits and liquid in one pan, and stir in the sugar over low heat until it is dissolved. Boil the mixture rapidly to setting point, then skim. Pour it into hot jars, then cover and label.

BLACKBERRY AND ELDERBERRY JAM

Metric/imperial		American
1kg/2 lb	elderberries	2 lb
1kg/2 lb	blackberries	2 lb
1.5kg/3 lb	sugar	6 cups

Wash the elderberries and strip them from their stalks. Wash the blackberries and remove any stems and unripe berries. Mix the two fruits together and simmer for about 20 minutes until the fruit is tender, crushing the berries with a wooden spoon to release their juices.

Stir in the sugar over low heat until it is dissolved, then boil the mixture rapidly to setting point. Skim the jam, then pour it into hot jars, cover and label.

BLACKBERRY JAM

Metric/imperial		American
3kg/6 lb	blackberries	6 lb
125ml/¼ pint	water	⅔ cup
4 × 5ml spoons/ 4 teaspoons	lemon juice	4 teaspoons
3kg/6 lb	sugar	12 cups

Wash the blackberries and remove any stems and unripe berries. Put the fruit into a pan with the water and lemon juice. Simmer until the fruit is very soft.

Stir in the sugar over low heat until dissolved. Boil the mixture rapidly to setting point, then skim. Pour the jam into hot jars, then cover and label.

BLACKCURRANT JAM

Metric/imperial		American
2kg/4 lb	blackcurrants	4 lb
1.5 litres/ 3 pints	water	1¾ quarts
3kg/6 lb	sugar	12 cups

Wash the fruit and remove the stems. Put the fruit into a pan with the water, and simmer gently until the fruit is soft, stirring often to prevent it burning.

Stir in the sugar over low heat until it is dissolved. Boil the mixture rapidly to setting point, then skim. Pour the jam into hot jars, then cover and label.

FRESH FIG JAM

Metric/imperial		American
1kg/2 lb	fresh figs	2 lb
500g/1 lb	cooking apples	1 lb
	grated rind of 2 lemons	
	juice of 6 lemons	
1kg/2 lb	sugar	4 cups

Wash and peel the figs, then blanch them in boiling water for 1 minute. Drain well, rinse in cold water, and slice thinly.

Peel, core and slice the apples. Mix with the figs, lemon rind and juice in a pan. Cover and simmer over low heat until the fruit is tender, stirring often.

Stir in the sugar over low heat until dissolved. Boil rapidly for 15 minutes to setting point, then skim. Pour the jam into hot jars, then cover and label.

Variation
For a spiced flavour, tie a small piece of cinnamon stick, a piece of bruised root ginger and 2 whole cloves into a piece of muslin, and add this to the pan while the fruit is softening. Remove the bag before bottling.

DAMSON JAM

Metric/imperial		American
1.5kg/3 lb	damsons	3 lb
375ml/¾ pint	water	2 cups
1.5kg/3 lb	sugar	6 cups

Wash the damsons, then simmer them in the water until they are soft, removing the stones as they rise in the pan.

Stir in the sugar over low heat until it is dissolved. Boil the mixture rapidly to setting point, then skim. Pour the jam into hot jars, then cover and label.

DAMSON AND PEAR JAM

Metric/imperial		American
1kg/2 lb	damsons	2 lb
1kg/2 lb	ripe pears	2 lb
250ml/½ pint	water	1¼ cups
2kg/4 lb	sugar	8 cups

Wash the damsons and put them into a pan. Peel and core the pears and add them to the damsons with the water. Simmer the fruit until soft, removing the damson stones as they rise to the surface.

Stir in the sugar over low heat until it is dissolved. Boil the mixture rapidly to setting point, them skim. Pour the jam into hot jars, then cover and label.

CHERRY JAM

Metric/imperial		American
2kg/4 lb	black cherries	4 lb
8g/¼ oz	citric **or** tartaric acid powder	1 teaspoon
1.5kg/3 lb	sugar	6 cups

Take the stones out of the cherries. Crack 24 of the stones and remove the kernels.

Put the cherries and the kernels into a pan with the acid. Cook over very low heat until there is enough juice to simmer and the fruit is very soft, stirring often to prevent burning.

Stir in the sugar over low heat until dissolved. Boil the mixture rapidly to setting point, then skim. Pour the jam into hot jars, then cover and label.

Note Do not expect a strong set from this jam.

GREENGAGE JAM

Metric/imperial		American
3kg/6 lb	greengages	6 lb
500ml/1 pint	water	2½ cups
3kg/6 lb	sugar	12 cups

Wash the greengages and cut them in half. Take out the stones. Put the fruit and water into a pan, and simmer until the fruit is soft.

Meanwhile, crack a few of the stones and remove the kernels. Blanch the kernels in boiling water and split them in half. Add the split kernels to the fruit while it is softening.

When soft, stir in the sugar over low heat until it has dissolved. Boil the mixture rapidly to setting point, then skim. Pour it into hot jars, then cover and label.

JAPONICA JAM

Metric/imperial		American
2kg/4 lb	japonica fruit	4 lb
3 litres/6 pints	water	3¾ quarts
	sugar	
2 × 5ml spoons/ 2 teaspoons	ground cloves	2 teaspoons

Wash the fruit, but do not peel or core it. Coarsely slice the fruit, then put it into a pan with the water, and simmer until soft.

Pass the mixture into a sieve, then weigh the sieved pulp, and allow an equal amount of sugar to the pulp.

Return the pulp to the pan, add the sugar and cloves, and stir over low heat until the sugar has dissolved. Boil rapidly to setting point, then skim. Pour the jam into hot jars, cover and label.

Note The ornamental japonica yields a hard fruit which is a type of quince and has a similar flavour.

MEDLAR JAM

Metric/imperial		American
2kg/4 lb	very ripe medlars	4 lb
	sugar	
	vanilla pod	

Scrape the pulp from the medlars, and cook very gently until soft, adding a little water if necessary so that they do not burn.

Sieve the pulp, then weigh it, allowing 375g/12 oz/¾ US cup sugar to each 500g/1 lb/1 US cup fruit pulp.

Return the pulp to the pan, add the sugar, and stir over low heat until it is dissolved.

Put in the vanilla pod, and boil rapidly to setting point, stirring well. Remove the vanilla pod, skim the jam, pour into hot jars, then cover and label.

Note Medlars are shaped like large rose-hips, and are the colour of unripe russet apples. They are very hard and should be gathered when fully formed, then kept for some weeks until soft and the flesh is brown.

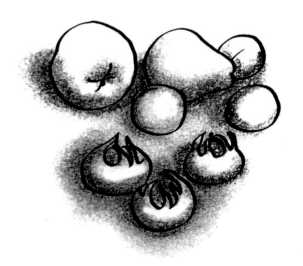

QUINCE JAM

Metric/imperial		American
2kg/4 lb	quinces	4 lb
	water	
	sugar	

Peel and core the quinces and cut the flesh into small cubes. Put them into a pan with just enough water to cook them without burning. Simmer until the fruit is soft but unbroken.

Weigh or measure the fruit and liquid, and allow 500g/1 lb/ 1 US cup sugar to each 500g/1 lb/1 US cup fruit and liquid. Stir together the sugar, fruit and liquid, and leave overnight.

Put the mixture into a pan and bring to the boil. Boil rapidly to setting point, then simmer for 20 minutes. Skim the jam, then pour into hot jars, cover and label.

Note Quince jam sets very quickly, so it may not be necessary to boil to setting point.

MULBERRY JAM

Metric/imperial		American
1kg/2 lb	mulberries	2 lb
	grated rind and juice of 1 lemon	
750g/1½ lb	sugar	3 cups

Rinse the mulberries gently so that no juice is lost. Put the wet berries into a pan over low heat, and simmer until the fruit is soft.

Add the lemon rind and juice, and stir in the sugar over low heat until dissolved. Boil the mixture rapidly to setting point, then skim. Pour the jam into hot jars, then cover and label.

PEACH JAM

Metric/imperial		American
1kg/2 lb	ripe peaches	2 lb
	juice of 1 lemon	
750g/1½ lb	sugar	3 cups
2 × 5ml spoons/ 2 teaspoons	rosewater	2 teaspoons
2 × 5ml spoons/ 2 teaspoons	orange flower water	2 teaspoons

Skin the peaches by dipping them first into boiling water and then into cold water. Cut the peaches in quarters and take out the stones.

Put the fruit into a pan with the lemon juice. Simmer gently until the fruit is soft, stirring frequently and adding a little water if necessary to prevent burning.

Stir in the sugar over low heat until it is dissolved, then boil the mixture rapidly to setting point. Stir in the rosewater and orange flower water, and simmer for 1 minute, then skim. Pour the jam into hot jars, then cover and label.

FRESH APRICOT JAM

Metric/imperial		American
3kg/6 lb	fresh apricots	6 lb
375ml/¾ pint	water	2 cups
	juice of 1 lemon	
3kg/6 lb	sugar	12 cups

Wash the apricots and cut them in half. Take out the stones. Put the fruit, water and lemon juice into a pan, and simmer until the fruit is soft.

Meanwhile, crack a few of the stones and remove the kernels. Blanch the kernels in boiling water and split them in half. Add the split kernels to the fruit while it is softening.

When soft, stir in the sugar over low heat until it has dissolved. Boil the mixture rapidly to setting point, then skim. Pour it into hot jars, then cover and label.

DRIED APRICOT JAM

Metric/imperial		American
500g/1 lb	dried apricots	1 lb
1.5 litres/ 3 pints	water	1¾ quarts
	juice of 1 lemon	
1.5kg/3 lb	sugar	6 cups
75g/3 oz	blanched almonds	⅔ cup

Cut the apricots into small pieces with scissors, and leave them to soak in the water for 24 hours.

Put the fruit and water into a pan, and cook gently for 30 minutes.

Add the lemon juice, sugar and almonds, halved, to the fruit, and stir over low heat until the sugar has dissolved. Boil the mixture rapidly to setting point, then skim. Pour it into hot jars, then cover and label.

GOOSEBERRY JAM

Metric/imperial		American
3kg/6 lb	slightly under-ripe gooseberries	6 lb
1 litre/2 pints	water	5 cups
3kg/6 lb	sugar	12 cups

Wash the gooseberries, top and tail them, then put them into a pan with the water. Simmer for about 30 minutes until soft, mashing and stirring well.

Stir in the sugar over low heat until dissolved. Boil the mixture rapidly to setting point, then skim. Pour it into hot jars, then cover and label.

Note The best gooseberries for jam are slightly under-ripe. Gooseberries which remain green when they are ripe will make a green jam if the fruit and sugar are cooked quickly together – prolonged boiling results in a reddish jam. Fully ripe or dessert gooseberries make a lightly setting pink jam.

Variation
For a delicate muscat flavour, tie a few elderflower heads in muslin, and add them to the pan while cooking the fruit in water. Remove the bag before bottling.

Fresh Apricot Jam

RASPBERRY JAM

Metric/imperial		American
25g/1 oz	butter	2 tablespoons
1.5 kg/3 lb	raspberries	3 lb
1.5kg/3 lb	sugar	6 cups

Warm a pan and rub it with butter. Put in the raspberries, and cook over very low heat until the juice runs. Meanwhile, warm the sugar in the oven.

Add the warmed sugar to the fruit, and cook over low heat for 30 minutes until dissolved. Skim, then pour into hot jars, cover and label.

Note Raspberry jam made in this way will keep a fresh red colour and will retain the flavour of fresh fruit. It does not set firmly.

RASPBERRY AND RHUBARB JAM

Metric/imperial		American
1.5kg/3 lb	raspberries	3 lb
1.5kg/3 lb	rhubarb	3 lb
250ml/½ pint	water	1¼ cups
3kg/6 lb	sugar	12 cups

Wash the raspberries. Wash the rhubarb and cut it into chunks, then put it into a pan with the water, and simmer until soft. Add the raspberries, and continue cooking until the raspberries are soft.

Stir the sugar into the fruit mixture over low heat until the sugar has dissolved, then boil rapidly to setting point. Skim, then pour the jam into hot jars, cover and label.

RASPBERRY AND REDCURRANT JAM

Metric/imperial		American
750g/1½ lb	raspberries	1½ lb
750g/1½ lb	redcurrants	1½ lb
500ml/1 pint	water	2½ cups
1.5kg/3 lb	sugar	6 cups

Wash the raspberries. Wash and string the redcurrants. Mix together the fruit in a pan with the water, and simmer for 20 minutes.

Stir in the sugar over low heat until dissolved. Boil the mixture rapidly to setting point, then skim. Pour it into hot jars, then cover and label.

RHUBARB AND FIG JAM

Metric/imperial		American
1kg/2 lb	rhubarb	2 lb
250g/8 oz	dried figs	8 oz
1kg/2 lb	sugar	4 cups
	juice of 1 lemon	

Wash the rhubarb and cut it into chunks. Cut the figs into small pieces. Mix the fruit, sugar and lemon juice in a bowl, and leave to stand for 24 hours.

Put the mixture into a pan and bring it to the boil. Boil rapidly to setting point, then cool for 15 minutes.

Stir the jam well to distribute the figs, then skim. Pour it into hot jars, then cover and label.

STRAWBERRY JAM

Metric/imperial		American
2kg/4 lb	strawberries	4 lb
1 × 5ml spoon/ 1 teaspoon	citric **or** tartaric acid powder	1 teaspoon
1.75kg/3½ lb	sugar	7 cups

Hull, pick over and wash the strawberries. Put them into a pan with the acid, and simmer for 30 minutes or until the fruit is soft.

Stir the sugar into the fruit over low heat until dissolved. Boil the mixture rapidly to setting point, then cool for 15 minutes.

Stir the jam well to distribute the fruit, then skim. Pour it into hot jars, then cover and label.

GREEN TOMATO JAM

Metric/imperial		American
1kg/2 lb	green tomatoes	2 lb
	rind of 1 orange	
750g/1½ lb	sugar	3 cups

Cut up the green tomatoes and put them into a pan. Shred or pare the orange rind into very fine strips, then simmer these in a little water until tender.

Drain the orange rind and add it to the tomatoes. Cook the tomatoes over low heat until they are tender.

Stir the sugar into the tomatoes over low heat until dissolved, then boil the mixture rapidly to setting point. Skim, then pour the jam into hot jars, cover and label.

SUMMER JAM

Metric/imperial		American
250g/8 oz	blackcurrants	8 oz
250g/8 oz	redcurrants	8 oz
250g/8 oz	raspberries	8 oz
250g/8 oz	strawberries	8 oz
125ml/¼ pint	water	⅔ cup
1kg/2 lb	sugar	4 cups

Pick over and wash all the fruit. Remove the stems of the blackcurrants and the redcurrants.

Put the blackcurrants into a pan with very little water, and simmer them until tender.

Add the remaining fruit, and simmer for 10 minutes, then stir in the sugar over low heat until dissolved. Boil the mixture rapidly to setting point, then skim. Pour it into hot jars, then cover and label.

PLUM AND APPLE JAM

Metric/imperial		American
1kg/2 lb	plums	2 lb
1kg/2 lb	cooking apples	2 lb
750ml/1½ pints	water	3¾ cups
1.5kg/3 lb	sugar	6 cups

Wash the plums, cut them in half and take out the stones. Peel, core and slice the apples. Put the fruit and water into a pan, and simmer until soft.

Stir in the sugar over low heat until dissolved. Boil the mixture rapidly to setting point, then skim. Pour it into hot jars, then cover and label.

PEAR GINGER JAM

Metric/imperial		American
2kg/4 lb	cooking pears	4 lb
2kg/4 lb	sugar	8 cups
2 × 5ml spoons/ 2 teaspoons	ground ginger	2 teaspoons
	grated rind and juice of 2 lemons	

Peel and core the pears. Chop the flesh finely or put it through a mincer, then mix the flesh with the sugar in a large bowl; leave overnight.

Put the pear mixture into a pan with the ginger and the lemon rind and juice. Simmer the mixture over low heat until the fruit is tender, stirring well. Boil rapidly to setting point, then skim. Pour the jam into hot jars, then cover and label.

PLUM JAM

Metric/imperial		American
3kg/6 lb	plums	6 lb
500ml/1 pint	water	2½ cups
3kg/6 lb	sugar	12 cups

Wash the plums, cut them in half and take out the stones. Put the fruit and water into a pan, and simmer until the fruit is very soft.

Meanwhile, crack a few of the stones and remove the kernels. Blanch the kernels in boiling water and split them in half. Add the split kernels to the fruit while it is softening.

When soft, stir in the sugar until it has dissolved. Boil the mixture rapidly to setting point, then skim. Pour it into hot jars, then cover and label.

Pear Ginger Jam

Uncooked Jam

Uncooked jam can be stored in a freezer for six months and will remain brightly coloured with the delicious smell of fresh fruit. Since the fruit is ripe and uncooked, it retains the maximum fresh fruit flavour. Ingredients must be measured carefully, and instructions followed closely. The jams contain a high proportion of sugar, and the yield for each 500g/1 lb of fruit is high. Liquid pectin is required for setting purposes regardless of the fruits' natural pectin content.

The jams are mixed and left to set before freezing. After the first five hours at room temperature, the jams should be put into a refrigerator to finish setting before storage in the freezer. They are best packed in small quantities in rigid containers with tight-fitting lids, allowing 1.25cm/½ inch headspace.

Freezer jam should be stored at −18°C/0°F or lower. Sometimes a white mould-like formation is noticeable when jam is removed from the freezer, but this is not harmful and will melt quickly at room temperature. Jams should be thawed for 1 hour before serving. After opening, they should be stored in the refrigerator and used up quickly. If uncooked jam is stiff, or if 'weeping' has occurred, it should be lightly stirred to soften and blend before serving.

Caster sugar is required but American readers should use American granulated sugar which is already more finely ground than its British counterpart.

FREEZER APRICOT JAM

Metric/imperial		American
750g/1½ lb	fresh apricots	1½ lb
1 × 5ml spoon/ 1 teaspoon	citric acid powder	1 teaspoon
1kg/2 lb	caster sugar	4 cups
100ml/4 fl oz	liquid pectin	½ cup

Quickly blanch the apricots, then peel off their skins and remove their stones.

Mash the fruit, and stir in the citric acid and sugar. Leave the mixture for 20 minutes, stirring occasionally.

Add the pectin to the mixture, and stir for 3 minutes. Put it into small containers, then cover and seal. Leave at room temperature for 5 hours.

Refrigerate the jam until it is jelled, about 24–48 hours.

Store the jam in the freezer, thawing it for 1 hour at room temperature before serving.

Variation
Substitute peaches for the apricots.

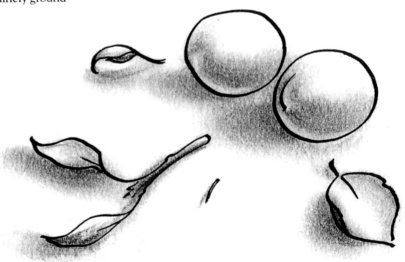

FREEZER CHERRY JAM

Metric/imperial		American
750g/1½ lb	Morello cherries	1½ lb
1kg/2 lb	caster sugar	4 cups
100ml/4 fl oz	liquid pectin	½ cup

Remove the stones from the cherries. Put the fruit through the coarse blade of a mincer or process very briefly in a food processor. The fruit should be coarsely chopped.

Stir the sugar into the fruit, and leave the mixture for 20 minutes, stirring occasionally.

Add the pectin to the fruit mixture, and stir for 3 minutes. Put it into small containers, cover and seal them, then leave for 5 hours at room temperature.

Refrigerate the jam until it is jelled, about 24–48 hours.

Store the jam in the freezer, thawing it for 1 hour at room temperature before serving.

FREEZER PLUM JAM

Metric/imperial		American
750g/1½ lb	Victoria **or** other dessert plums	1½ lb
1kg/2 lb	caster sugar	4 cups
2 × 5ml spoons/ 2 teaspoons	lemon juice	2 teaspoons
100ml/4 fl oz	liquid pectin	½ cup

Remove the stones from the plums, and stir in the sugar and the lemon juice. Leave the mixture for 20 minutes, stirring occasionally.

Add the pectin, and stir the mixture for 3 minutes. Put it into small containers, then cover and seal. Leave them for 5 hours at room temperature.

Refrigerate the jam until it is jelled, about 24–48 hours.

Store the jam in the freezer, thawing for 1 hour at room temperature before serving.

FREEZER RASPBERRY JAM

Metric/imperial		American
750g/1½ lb	raspberries	1½ lb
1.5kg/3 lb	caster sugar	6 cups
100ml/4 fl oz	liquid pectin	½ cup

Mash or sieve the fruit and stir the sugar into it. Leave the mixture for 20 minutes, stirring occasionally.

Add the pectin, and stir the mixture for 3 minutes. Put it into small containers, then cover and seal. Leave for 5 hours at room temperature.

Refrigerate the jam until it is jelled, about 24–48 hours.

Store the jam in the freezer, thawing it for 1 hour at room temperature before serving.

FREEZER STRAWBERRY JAM

Metric/imperial		American
750g/1½ lb	strawberries	1½ lb
1kg/2 lb	caster sugar	4 cups
100ml/4 fl oz	liquid pectin	½ cup

Hull and pick over the strawberries. Mash them and stir in the sugar. Leave the mixture for 20 minutes, stirring occasionally.

Add the pectin, and stir the mixture for 3 minutes. Put it into small containers, then cover and seal. Leave at room temperature for 5 hours.

Refrigerate the jam until it is jelled, about 24–48 hours.

Store the jam in the freezer, thawing it for 1 hour at room temperature before serving.

FREEZER BLACKBERRY JAM

Metric/imperial		American
750g/1½ lb	blackberries	1½ lb
1.37kg/2¾ lb	caster sugar	5½ cups
100ml/4 fl oz	liquid pectin	½ cup

Mash the blackberries and stir in the sugar. Leave them for 20 minutes, stirring occasionally.

Add the pectin, and stir the mixture for 3 minutes. Put it into small containers, then cover and seal. Leave at room temperature for 5 hours.

Refrigerate the jam until it is jelled, about 24–48 hours.

Store the jam in the freezer, thawing it for 1 hour at room temperature before serving.

Freezer jams should be frozen in rigid containers with tight-fitting lids

Marmalades

Citrus fruit marmalade is a delicious preserve easily made at home. All types of citrus fruit are suitable, particularly bitter Seville oranges, sweet oranges, grapefruit and tangerines. Seville oranges have a very short season, so it is worth freezing them for later use. They need only be wiped and packed in 1kg/2 lb bags. When needed for marmalade-making, they can be treated in exactly the same way as fresh fruit.

Equipment, sugar type and the general cooking method do not differ greatly from that of jams, but the fruit or peel (rind) should be sliced either manually or with a mixer or food processor. If the fruit has a great deal of pith, the peel and pith should be removed separately before slicing. Thin-skinned oranges and lemons can be cut into quarters lengthways without peeling, and the fruit and peel sliced through into thin slices.

Pips, pith and any trimmings should be put into a piece of muslin, then tied into a bag shape, and put into the pan during the first cooking. Valuable pectin is contained in this mixture. It should be removed and all liquid squeezed into the pan before the sugar is added.

The fruit should then be simmered in water until soft before boiling rapidly with sugar to setting point as for jams – a pressure cooker will help to speed up this initial cooking time (see page 31). When the peel (rind) is cooked, it should be completely soft when tested with the fingers. The liquid in this first cooking must be evaporated, and, generally, the contents of the pan will be reduced by almost half. After skimming, the mixture should be left for at least 5 minutes before stirring and pouring into jars as for jams.

Seville Orange Marmalade

Metric/imperial		American
1kg/2 lb	Seville oranges	2 lb
2 litres/4 pints	water	2½ quarts
	juice of 1 lemon	
2kg/4 lb	sugar	8 cups

Wipe the oranges, then cut them in half. Squeeze out the juice and pips. Tie the pips in a piece of muslin and put it in a pan. Put the orange juice in the pan with the water and juice of the lemon.

Slice the orange peel (rind) thinly and add it to the pan. Simmer the mixture for about 1½ hours or until the peel is soft and the liquid is reduced by half.

Remove the bag of pips, and squeeze any juice out of it into the pan. Stir in the sugar over low heat until dissolved. Boil the mixture rapidly to setting point, then skim. Cool the marmalade for about 15 minutes in the pan.

Stir the marmalade well, then pour it into hot jars, cover and label.

Chunky Whisky Marmalade

Metric/imperial		American
1.5kg/3 lb	Seville oranges	3 lb
2.5 litres/ 5 pints	water	3 quarts
	juice of 1 lemon	
3kg/6 lb	sugar	12 cups
1 × 15ml spoon/ 1 tablespoon	black treacle (molasses)	1 tablespoon
4 × 15ml spoons/ 4 tablespoons	Scotch whisky	4 tablespoons

Wipe the oranges, then cut them in half. Squeeze out the juice and pips. Tie the pips in a piece of muslin and put it in a pan. Put the juice into the pan with the water and lemon juice.

Cut the squeezed fruit and its peel (rind) into thick shreds, and add them to the pan. Simmer the mixture for about 1½ hours or until the peel is tender.

Remove the bag of pips, and squeeze any juice out of it into the pan. Stir in the sugar and treacle (molasses) over low heat until dissolved, then boil the mixture rapidly to setting point. Skim, then cool the marmalade for about 15 minutes in the pan.

Stir in the whisky, then pour the marmalade into hot jars, cover and label.

Orange Shred Marmalade

Metric/imperial		American
1kg/2 lb	Seville oranges	2 lb
2.5 litres/ 5 pints	water	3 quarts
	juice of 2 lemons	
1.5kg/3 lb	sugar	6 cups

Peel enough orange peel from the oranges to weigh 125g/4 oz, 2–3 oranges, then cut the rind into thin strips.

Cut up the fruit with the remaining peel attached, and put it into a pan with half the water and all the lemon juice. Cover the pan, and simmer the mixture for 2 hours.

Meanwhile, simmer the thin strips of peel in 500ml/1 pint/ 2½ US cups water until the rind is soft. Strain the liquid into the simmering fruit, and reserve the peel.

Strain the simmered fruit pulp through a jelly bag, and leave it to drip for 15 minutes.·

Reserve the strained liquid, and put the fruit pulp back into the pan. Add the remaining water, then simmer for 20 minutes, and strain the mixture through a jelly bag overnight.

Mix together the two liquids in a pan, then stir in the sugar over low heat until dissolved. Add the reserved peel, and boil rapidly to setting point. Skim the marmalade, then cool for 5 minutes in the pan.

Stir the marmalade well, then pour it into hot jars, cover and label.

GINGER MARMALADE

Metric/imperial		American
	5 Seville oranges	
2.5 litres/ 5 pints	water	3 quarts
1.5kg/3 lb	cooking apples	3 lb
3kg/6 lb	sugar	12 cups
250g/8 oz	crystallized ginger, chopped	1 cup
15g/½ oz	ground ginger	1 tablespoon

Cut the oranges in half and squeeze out the juice. Cut up the flesh and shred the peel (rind) finely. Put the orange peel and flesh, juice and the water into a pan. Tie the pips in a piece of muslin, put it in the pan and simmer the mixture for 1½ hours.

Remove the bag of pips, and squeeze any juice out of it into the pan.

Peel, core and slice the apples, then cook them in 4 × 15ml spoons/4 tablespoons water over low heat until the apple has turned to pulp.

Stir together the apples and simmered oranges, and stir in the sugar over low heat until dissolved. Add the chopped ginger with the ground ginger to the pan. Boil the mixture rapidly to setting point, then skim. Leave to cool for 5 minutes in the pan.

Stir the marmalade well, then pour it into hot jars, cover and label.

GRAPEFRUIT MARMALADE

Metric/imperial		American
	3 grapefruit	
	4 lemons	
2.4 litres/ 4 pints	water	2½ quarts
1.5kg/3 lb	sugar	6 cups

Cut all the fruit in half and squeeze out the juice. Take out the pips. Remove the white pith and membranes from the grapefruit. Tie the pips, pith and membranes in a piece of muslin, and put in a pan.

Shred all the fruit peel (rind) finely and cut up the flesh roughly. Put the peel, flesh and the water into a pan with the bag of pips, and simmer for 1½ hours.

Remove the bag of pips, and squeeze any juice out of it into the pan. Stir in the sugar over low heat until dissolved, then boil the mixture rapidly to setting point. Skim the marmalade, then leave to cool for 10 minutes in the pan.

Stir the marmalade well, then pour it into hot jars, cover and label.

Grapefruit Marmalade

Grapefruit Marmalade
Grapefruit Marmalade
Grapefruit Marmalade
JAFFA
JAFFA

LEMON MARMALADE

Metric/imperial		American
	8 large lemons	
4 litres/8 pints	water	5 quarts
	sugar	

Peel the lemons very finely and cut the peel (rind) into very fine shreds.

Remove the white pith and pips, tie them in a piece of muslin and put it in a pan with the shredded peel. Cut up the flesh of the lemons and put it into the pan with the peel and the water. Simmer the mixture for 1½ hours.

Remove the bag of pips, and squeeze any juice out of it into the pan. Weigh (measure) the contents of the pan and add an equal weight (quantity) of sugar. Stir in the sugar over low heat until dissolved, then boil rapidly to setting point. Skim the marmalade, then cool for 5 minutes in the pan.

Stir the marmalade well, then pour it into hot jars, cover and label.

LEMON AND LIME MARMALADE

Metric/imperial		American
	5 large lemons	
	3 limes	
3 litres/6 pints	water	3¾ quarts
	sugar	

Peel the lemons and limes thinly and cut the peel (rind) into fine shreds. Cover the peel with 500ml/1 pint/2½ US cups of the water, and simmer, covered, until soft.

Meanwhile, take all the white pith off the lemons and limes, and cut up the flesh. Put in a pan with the remaining water, then cover and simmer gently for 1½ hours until the fruit is soft.

Drain the shreds, reserving them and pouring the liquid into the simmering fruit. When the fruit is soft, strain it through a jelly bag.

Measure the liquid and allow 500g/1 lb/1 US cup sugar to each 500ml/1 pint/1 US cup liquid. Put the sugar, liquid and peel into a pan, and stir over low heat until the sugar has dissolved. Boil rapidly to setting point, then skim. Leave to cool for 5 minutes in the pan.

Stir the marmalade well, then pour it into hot jars, cover and label.

TANGERINE MARMALADE

Metric/imperial		American
1kg/2 lb	tangerines	2 lb
2.5 litres/ 5 pints	water	3 quarts
	1 grapefruit	
	1 lemon	
2 × 5ml spoons/ 2 teaspoons	tartaric acid powder	2 teaspoons
1.5kg/3 lb	sugar	6 cups

Peel the tangerines and cut the peel (rind) into fine shreds. Put them into a pan with 500ml/1 pint/2½ US cups water, and simmer for 30 minutes.

Peel the grapefruit and lemon, and mince or finely chop the peel. Chop the tangerine, grapefruit and lemon flesh, and put it into a pan with the minced or finely chopped peel, the water and acid. Simmer the mixture for 1½ hours.

Strain and reserve the tangerine peel, adding the liquid to the simmering fruit pulp. When the pulp is cooked, strain it and the simmering liquid through a jelly bag.

Discard the pulp, and return the strained juice to the pan. Stir in the sugar over low heat until dissolved. Add the reserved tangerine peel, and boil rapidly to setting point. Skim the marmalade, then leave to cool for 5 minutes in the pan.

Stir the marmalade well, then pour it into hot jars, cover and label.

PRESSURE COOKER MARMALADE

Metric/imperial		American
1kg/2 lb	Seville oranges	2 lb
	juice of 2 lemons	
1 litre/2 pints	water	5 cups
2kg/4 lb	sugar	8 cups

Peel the oranges and cut the peel (rind) into thin strips. Cut the white pith from the fruit, and tie it with the pips in a piece of muslin. Cut the fruit up roughly. Put the fruit, peel, lemon juice and the muslin bag into a pressure cooker with half the water. Bring the pan to 5kg/10 lb (medium) pressure, and cook for 10 minutes.

Reduce the pressure at room temperature. Remove the bag of pips, and squeeze any juice out of it into the pan. Add the remaining water and the sugar to the open pan, and heat gently, stirring well until the sugar has dissolved. Boil rapidly to setting point, then skim the marmalade. Leave to cool for 5 minutes in the pan.

Stir the marmalade well, then pour it into hot jars, cover and label.

JELLIES

Jelly-making is a little more complicated than jam-making, but the results are very rewarding – a sparkling clear jelly with a bright colour and fresh fruit flavour.

The only special equipment necessary is a jelly bag. A specially made flannel bag can be obtained at good kitchen or hardware shops, but a bag can be made from a double layer of muslin tied with string. The jelly bag can be suspended on a special stand or between the legs of an upturned chair.

Basic Method

Wash all fruit, which should be ripe but not over-ripe. Hard fruit such as apples and quinces should be sliced without peeling and coring; stone fruit should be cut in half, and soft fruit can be left on stems if these are clean. Crush the fruit lightly in the preserving pan with a spoon to start the juices flowing. A small proportion (about one-third) of slightly under-ripe fruit will help to give a good set. Apples, redcurrants and gooseberries are rich in pectin, so they can be mixed with other fruit such as raspberries and strawberries which do not set well on their own.

Some berries and currants need no water, but blackcurrants and hard fruits need water to help soften their skins. If the fruit is not a very juicy one, cook it very gently so that the juices run but do not dry out.

When the fruit is soft and the juices extracted, strain the pulp through the jelly bag, and drip slowly into a bowl; this may take an hour or two, or overnight. Never be tempted to squeeze, stir or shake the fruit pulp as this will make the jelly cloudy.

Measure the liquid, allowing generally 500g/1 lb/1 US cup sugar to each 500ml/1 pint/1 US cup juice for fruit rich in pectin and acid, but 375g/12 oz/¾ US cup sugar to each 500ml/1 pint/1 US cup juice for fruit with a poorer setting quality. As with jams, warmed sugar will, in most cases, speed up the dissolving process. Apple and gooseberry jellies, however, keep a better colour if cold sugar is added to cold juice.

Once the sugar has dissolved, boil the jelly rapidly to setting point. The temperature and flake tests on page 9 are most recommended. Skim the jelly with a metal spoon dipped in boiling water, then pour into small hot jars, tilting the jars so that the jelly does not form air bubbles. Cover at once with waxed paper circles, then cover completely or when cold, but do not move the jelly until it has set. Label when cold. Be sure to store the jelly in a cool, dry place.

Preserving Faults

Do not leave the strained fruit juice too long before cooking as this can affect the setting quality of the jelly.

Cloudy jelly will result from either poorly strained juice through a bag which is too thin, or from pulp which has been forced through the bag rather than being left to drip by itself.

BLACKCURRANT JELLY

Metric/imperial		American
2kg/4 lb	blackcurrants	4 lb
1.5 litres/3 pints	water	1¾ quarts
	sugar	

Wash the fruit and remove any stems and leaves. Simmer the blackcurrants in the water for 1 hour or until soft.

Strain the mixture through a jelly bag and discard the pulp. Measure the juice and allow 500g/1 lb/1 US cup sugar to each 500ml/1 pint/1 US cup liquid. Heat the juice gently, stirring in the sugar until it is dissolved. Boil the mixture rapidly to setting point, then skim.

Pour the jelly into small, hot jars, then cover. Label when cold.

APPLE JELLY

Metric/imperial		American
3kg/6 lb	cooking apples (see **Note**)	6 lb
	juice of 2 lemons	
	sugar	

Wash the apples and remove any bruised or damaged pieces before weighing. Do not peel or core the apples, but cut them into pieces, and put them into a pan with the lemon juice and enough water to cover. Simmer until the apples are soft and the liquid is reduced by about one-third.

Strain the mixture through a jelly bag and discard the pulp. Measure the liquid and allow 500g/1 lb/1 US cup sugar to each 500ml/1 pint/1 US cup liquid.

Add the sugar to the cold strained liquid, and bring the mixture to the boil, stirring until the sugar has dissolved. Boil rapidly to setting point, then skim.

Pour the jelly into small, hot jars, and cover. Label when cold.

Note A mixture of apples can be used for the jelly, and/or windfalls, but damaged and bruised pieces must be carefully cut away.

Use apple jelly as the basis of a herb jelly (see page 40) to eat with meat.

Variations
1) For a rich red colour, add a few blackberries, cranberries, redcurrants or raspberries to the apples.
2) Simmer two rose-geranium leaves with the apples to obtain a deliciously scented jelly.

APPLE AND BLACKBERRY JELLY

Metric/imperial		American
2kg/4 lb	blackberries	4 lb
1kg/2 lb	cooking apples	2 lb
1 litre/2 pints	water	5 cups
	sugar	

Wash the blackberries and remove any stems and unripe berries. Put the blackberries into a pan. Wash the apples and cut them up without peeling or coring. Mix the apples with the blackberries and the water, and simmer for about 1 hour until the fruit is soft.

Strain the mixture through a jelly bag and discard the pulp. Measure the liquid and allow 500g/1 lb/1 US cup sugar to each 500ml/1 pint/1 US cup liquid. Heat the juice gently, stirring in the sugar until it is dissolved. Boil the mixture rapidly to setting point, then skim.

Pour the jelly into small, hot jars, and cover. Label when cold.

CRAB-APPLE JELLY

Metric/imperial		American
2kg/4 lb	crab-apples	4 lb
1 litre/2 pints	water	5 cups
	6 cloves	
	sugar	

Wash the fruit and remove any damaged or bruised pieces. Do not peel or core the fruit, but cut it in quarters. Put the fruit into a pan with the water and cloves. Bring the mixture to the boil, then simmer until the apples are very soft. It may be necessary to add a little more water if the fruit begins to boil dry.

Strain the mixture through a jelly bag and discard the pulp. Measure the liquid and allow 500g/1 lb/1 us cup sugar to each 500ml/1 pint/1 us cup liquid. Heat the juice gently, stirring in the sugar until it is dissolved. Boil the mixture rapidly to setting point, then skim.

Pour the jelly into small, hot jars, then cover. Label when cold.

GOOSEBERRY JELLY

Metric/imperial		American
2kg/4 lb	green gooseberries	4 lb
	sugar	

Wash the gooseberries and top and tail them. Put the fruit into a pan with just enough water to cover, and simmer for about 1 hour until the fruit is soft.

Strain the mixture through a jelly bag and discard the pulp. Measure the liquid and allow 500g/1 lb/1 us cup sugar to each 500ml/1 pint/1 us cup liquid.

Add the sugar to the cold strained liquid, and bring the mixture to the boil, stirring until the sugar has dissolved. Boil rapidly to setting point, then skim.

Pour the jelly into small, hot jars, then cover. Label when cold.

Variation
A flavour of muscat grapes will be imparted to the jelly if a bunch of elderflower heads is tied into muslin and added to the juice while it cooks with the sugar.

CRANBERRY JELLY

Metric/imperial		American
1kg/2 lb	cranberries	2 lb
500ml/1 pint	water	2½ cups
	sugar	

Cook the cranberries very gently in the water until the fruit is tender.

Strain the mixture through a jelly bag, and discard the pulp. Measure the liquid and allow 500g/1 lb/1 us cup sugar to each 500ml/1 pint/1 us cup liquid. Heat the juice gently, stirring in the sugar until it is dissolved. Boil the mixture rapidly to setting point, then skim.

Pour the jelly into small, hot jars, and cover. Label when cold.

Note This jelly is good served with turkey, chicken or game.

SUMMER JELLY

Metric/imperial		American
500g/1 lb	redcurrants	1 lb
500g/1 lb	raspberries	1 lb
500g/1 lb	strawberries	1 lb
500g/1 lb	black cherries	1 lb
1 × 5ml spoon/ 1 teaspoon	tartaric acid powder	1 teaspoon
500ml/1 pint	water	2½ cups
	sugar	

Put the fruit into a pan with the tartaric acid and water, and simmer until the fruit is soft.

Strain the mixture through a jelly bag and discard the pulp. Measure the juice and allow 500g/1 lb/1 US cup sugar to each 500ml/1 pint/1 US cup juice. Heat the juice gently, stirring in the sugar until it is dissolved. Boil the mixture rapidly to setting point, then skim.

Pour the jelly into small, hot jars, then cover. Label when cold.

AUTUMN JELLY

Metric/imperial		American
1.5kg/3 lb	elderberries	3 lb
500g/1 lb	cooking apples	1 lb
500g/1 lb	damsons	1 lb
500g/1 lb	blackberries	1 lb
1 litre/2 pints	water	5 cups
1 × 5ml spoon/ 1 teaspoon	ground cloves	1 teaspoon
1 × 5ml spoon/ 1 teaspoon	ground allspice	1 teaspoon
1 × 2.5ml spoon/ ½ teaspoon	ground ginger	½ teaspoon
	a pinch of ground cinnamon	
	sugar	

Pick the elderberries from their stalks. Do not core or peel the apples, but cut them into pieces. Mix the pieces with the elderberries, damsons and blackberries in a pan with the water and spices. Simmer for about 1 hour until the fruit is soft.

Strain the mixture through a jelly bag and discard the pulp. Measure the liquid and allow 500g/1 lb/1 US cup sugar to each 500ml/1 pint/1 US cup liquid. Heat the juice gently, stirring in the sugar until it is dissolved. Boil the mixture rapidly to setting point, then skim.

Pour the jelly into small, hot jars, then cover. Label when cold.

BLACKBERRY OR BRAMBLE JELLY

Metric/imperial		American
2kg/4 lb	blackberries (see **Note**)	4 lb
	juice of 2 lemons	
250ml/½ pint	water	1¼ cups
	sugar	

Wash the blackberries well and discard unripe fruit and stems. Put the berries into a pan with the lemon juice and water, and simmer for 1 hour until the fruit is soft.

Strain the mixture through a jelly bag and discard the pulp. Measure the juice and allow 500g/1 lb/1 US cup sugar to each 500ml/1 pint/1 US cup liquid. Heat the juice gently, stirring in the sugar until it is dissolved. Boil the mixture rapidly to setting point, then skim.

Pour the jelly into small, hot jars, then cover. Label when cold.

Note Use slightly under-ripe berries for this jelly.

Variation
A pinch of ground mace, nutmeg and cinnamon can be added after skimming the jelly.

This spiced jelly is delicious when served with meat.

JAPONICA JELLY

Metric/imperial		American
1.5kg/3 lb	japonica fruit	3 lb
4 × 15ml spoons/ 4 tablespoons	lemon juice	4 tablespoons
3 litres/6 pints	water	3¾ quarts
	sugar	

Wash the fruit but do not peel or core it. Cut the japonica fruit into pieces, and put them into a pan with the lemon juice and water. Simmer for about 1 hour until the fruit is soft.

Strain the mixture through a jelly bag and discard the pulp. Measure the liquid and allow 500g/1 lb/1 US cup sugar to each 500ml/1 pint/1 US cup liquid. Heat the juice gently, stirring in the sugar until it is dissolved. Boil the mixture rapidly to setting point, then skim.

Pour the jelly into small, hot jars, then cover. Label when cold.

Note The ornamental japonica shrub yields a very hard fruit which is a type of quince and which produces a jam with a flavour similar to quince.

Bramble Jelly

Granulated Sugar

Bramble Jelly

RASPBERRY AND REDCURRANT JELLY

Metric/imperial		American
1kg/2 lb	redcurrants	2 lb
1kg/2 lb	raspberries	2 lb
500ml/1 pint	water	2½ cups
	sugar	

Strip the redcurrants from their stems. Put them into a pan with the raspberries and water, and cook gently until the fruit is very soft.

Strain the mixture through a jelly bag and discard the pulp. Measure the juice and allow 500g/1 lb/1 us cup sugar to each 500ml/1 pint/1 us cup liquid. Heat the juice gently, stirring in the sugar until it is dissolved. Boil the mixture rapidly to setting point, then skim.

Pour the jelly into small, hot jars, then cover. Label when cold.

Note The redcurrants ensure that the jelly will have a good set but the flavour of raspberries also comes through.

This is a good jelly for glazing fruit flans or tarts.

REDCURRANT JELLY

Metric/imperial		American
1.5kg/3 lb	redcurrants	3 lb
500ml/1 pint	water	2½ cups
	sugar	

Strip the redcurrants from their stems. Put the fruit and water in a pan, and simmer gently until the fruit is very soft.

Strain the mixture through a jelly bag and discard the pulp. Measure the liquid and allow 500g/1 lb/1 us cup sugar to 500ml/1 pint/1 us cup liquid. Heat the juice gently, stirring in the sugar until it is dissolved. Boil the mixture rapidly to setting point, then skim.

Pour the jelly into small, hot jars, and cover, but work quickly as this jelly sets quickly. Label the jars when cold.

Note This jelly is especially good with lamb, hare or other game.

Variation
Spiced Redcurrant Jelly
Make as for Redcurrant Jelly, but add 125ml/¼ pint/⅔ us cup white vinegar to the liquid. Tie ½ cinnamon stick and 3 cloves in a piece of muslin to cook with the fruit, and remove it when the mixture is put through the jelly bag.

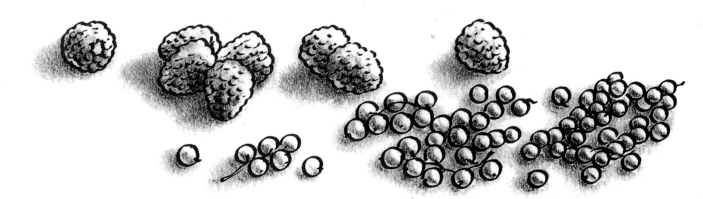

STRAWBERRY AND REDCURRANT JELLY

Metric/imperial		American
500g/1 lb	strawberries	1 lb
250g/8 oz	redcurrants	8 oz
4 × 15ml spoons/ 4 tablespoons	water	4 tablespoons
	sugar	

Hull the strawberries and remove the stems from the redcurrants. Put the fruit into a pan with the water, and cook over low heat until very soft.

Strain the mixture through a jelly bag and discard the pulp. Measure the juice and allow 500g/1 lb/1 US cup sugar to each 500ml/1 pint/1 US cup liquid. Heat the juice gently, stirring in the sugar until it is dissolved. Boil the mixture rapidly to setting point, then skim.

Pour the jelly into small, hot jars, then cover. Label when cold.

LEMON JELLY

Metric/imperial		American
	6 large lemons	
1.5 litres/ 3 pints	water	1¾ quarts
	sugar	

Wipe the lemons but do not peel them. Slice them thinly and remove the pips. Put the fruit into a pan with the water. Tie the pips in a piece of muslin, put it in the pan and simmer the mixture for 1½ hours.

Remove the bag of pips, then strain the mixture through a jelly bag and discard the pulp. Measure the liquid and allow 500g/1 lb/ 1 US cup sugar to each 500ml/1 pint/1 US cup liquid.

Bring the lemon liquid to boiling point, then stir in the sugar until dissolved. Boil rapidly to setting point, then skim.

Pour the jelly into small, hot jars, and cover. Label when cold.

ORANGE JELLY

Metric/imperial		American
500ml/1 pint	orange juice	2½ cups
	juice of 2 lemons	
250ml/½ pint	water	1¼ cups
875g/1¾ lb	sugar	1¾ lb

Strain both the orange and lemon juices. Put into a pan with the water, and boil for 10 minutes. Stir in the sugar over low heat until dissolved, then boil rapidly to setting point.

Pour the jelly into small, hot jars, and cover. Label when cold.

MINT JELLY

cooking apples	
white vinegar	
fresh mint	
sugar	
green food colouring	

Wash the apples but do not peel or core them. Cut them into pieces and put into a pan. Using three parts water to one part white vinegar, add liquid to the pan so that it just covers the apples. Add a large bunch of washed mint, and simmer until the fruit is very soft.

Strain the mixture through a jelly bag and discard the pulp. Measure the liquid and allow 500g/1 lb/1 us cup sugar to 500ml/ 1 pint/1 us cup liquid. Heat the juice gently, stirring in the sugar until it is dissolved. Boil the mixture rapidly to setting point. Just before removing the jelly from the heat, add some finely chopped fresh mint leaves and a few drops of green food colouring. Skim the jelly well, cool slightly, then stir it well.

Pour the jelly into small hot jars, then cover and label.

Note Serve with roast lamb.

Variations

Alternative Mint Jelly
Substitute gooseberries or redcurrants for the apples.

Sage, Parsley and Thyme Jellies
Make as for Mint Jelly, using either apples or gooseberries. Replace the mint with the herb of your choice.

Serve with duck, pork or ham.

TOMATO JELLY

Metric/imperial		American
1.5kg/3 lb	red tomatoes	3 lb
3 × 15ml spoons/ 3 tablespoons	lemon juice	3 tablespoons
	½ cinnamon stick	
750g/1½ lb	sugar	3 cups

Wipe the tomatoes and cut them into pieces. Put them in a pan and simmer over very low heat until soft.

Strain the tomatoes through a jelly bag and discard the pulp. Heat the juice with the lemon juice and cinnamon to boiling point, stirring in the sugar until it is dissolved. Boil the mixture rapidly to setting point, then remove the cinnamon stick. Skim the jelly, then pour it into small, hot jars, and cover. Label when cold.

Note Serve this unusual jelly with cream cheese, ham or poultry.

Jellies should be sparkling clear with a bright colour

MEDLAR JELLY

Metric/imperial		American
1kg/2 lb	very ripe medlars	2 lb
	1 lemon	
	sugar	

Peel the medlars, and remove the pips. Slice the flesh into a pan with enough water to cover. Cut up the lemon without peeling, and add to the pan. Simmer until the fruit is soft.

Strain the mixture through a jelly bag and discard the pulp. Measure the liquid and allow 375g/12 oz/¾ US cup sugar to each 500ml/1 pint/1 US cup liquid. Heat the juice gently, stirring in the sugar until dissolved. Boil the mixture rapidly to setting point, then skim.

Pour the jelly into hot jars, then cover. Label when cold.

Note Medlar jelly may be eaten as a spread, but is delicious as an accompaniment to game.

QUINCE JELLY

Metric/imperial		American
2kg/4 lb	quinces	4 lb
3 litres/6 pints	water	3¾ quarts
	sugar	

Wash the quinces but do not peel or core them. Cut them up into small pieces and put them into a pan with two-thirds of the water. Cover the pan and simmer for 1 hour or until the fruit is soft.

Strain off the cooking liquid and reserve it. Add the remaining water to the pulp, and simmer for 30 minutes.

Strain off the cooking liquid and mix it with the reserved liquid. Discard the pulp. Measure the liquid and allow 500g/1 lb/1 US cup sugar to each 500ml/1 pint/1 US cup liquid. Heat the juice gently, stirring in the sugar until it is dissolved. Boil the mixture rapidly to setting point, then skim.

Pour the jelly into small, hot jars, then cover. Label when cold.

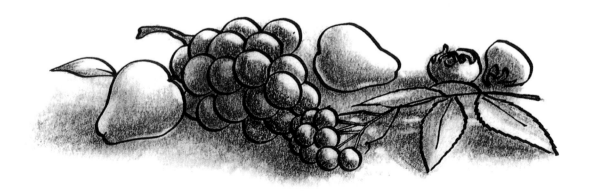

GRAPE JELLY

unripe grape thinnings (see **Note**)	
sugar	

Wash the grapes, put them into a pan with enough water to cover, and simmer until soft.

Strain the fruit through a jelly bag and discard the pulp. Measure the juice and allow 500g/1 lb/1 US cup sugar to each 500ml/1 pint/1 US cup juice. Heat the juice gently, stirring in the sugar until it is dissolved. Boil the mixture to setting point, then skim.

Pour the jelly into small, hot jars, and cover. Label when cold.

Note The grapes should be no larger than peas.

ROWAN-BERRY JELLY

Metric/imperial		American
2kg/4 lb	rowan-berries	4 lb
4 × 15ml spoons/ 4 tablespoons	lemon juice	4 tablespoons
750ml/1½ pints	water	3¾ cups
	sugar	

Remove the rowan-berries from their stems and put the fruit into a pan with the lemon juice and water. Simmer the mixture for 45 minutes or until the fruit is soft.

Strain the mixture through a jelly bag and discard the pulp. Measure the liquid and allow 500g/1 lb/1 US cup sugar to each 500ml/1 pint/1 US cup liquid. Heat the juice gently, stirring in the sugar until it is dissolved. Boil the mixture rapidly to setting point, then skim.

Pour the jelly into small, hot jars, then cover. Label when cold.

Note Serve this jelly with lamb, venison and other game.

Fruit Curds, Butters and Cheeses

Fruit curds are creamy fruit mixtures made with fresh fruit, eggs, butter and sugar. They are best made in small quantities and packaged in small jars (for cupboard storage – 2 months) or small freezer containers (6 months).

Caster sugar (see page 22) and unsalted butter should be used. Eggs are best strained before adding to the mixture as this ensures a smooth texture.

Curds should be cooked in a double saucepan (double boiler) or in a heatproof bowl over hot water, and the cooking heat should be low. The mixture must be stirred well during cooking, and, when ready, will be creamy and coat the back of a spoon. It will thicken as it cools.

Curds are delicious for tart and cake fillings and spreads, or may be used as sauces for ices or puddings.

Fruit butters and cheeses are thick mixtures of fruit pulp and sugar, but they vary slightly. *Fruit butter* should be thick but not completely set, with the consistency of thick cream so that it can be spread on bread or toast. *Fruit cheese* is much firmer and is eaten sliced with cream or milk puddings, savoury dishes or light snacks.

Large quantities of fruit or windfalls can be used up in making *butters* or *cheeses*, as these quantities reduce considerably during cooking. *Fruit butter* usually contains half the amount of sugar and fruit pulp. Brown sugar gives a good flavour, but darkens the preserve. Ground spices also darken the preserve, so it might be better to use whole spices tied in muslin. A little lemon juice will sharpen and improve fruit flavours.

The preserves should be tested on a plate for setting point. *Fruit butter* is ready when no rim of liquid appears round the edge of the mixture. *Fruit cheese* should be much firmer and will be ready when a spoon drawn across the bottom of the pan leaves a clear line. Both *butters* and *cheeses* should look thick and glossy. Put them into small, hot jars which can be used up quickly, and use wide-mouthed straight-sided jars for *cheeses* so that they can be turned out easily.

Lemon Curd

Metric/imperial		American
	4 large lemons	
175g/6 oz	butter	¾ cup
500g/1 lb	caster sugar	2 cups
	4 eggs	

Grate the lemon rind finely, squeeze out the juice and strain it.

Melt the butter in a heatproof bowl over barely simmering water or in the top of a double saucepan (double boiler). Add the lemon rind, strained juice and the sugar, and stir until the sugar has dissolved.

Beat the eggs well and add them to the mixture. Cook gently over barely simmering water, stirring well, until the mixture thickens.

Pour the curd into small, hot jars, and cover. Alternatively, cool, then pour into small freezer containers, and freeze.

Lemon and Lime Marmalade (page 30), Chunky Whisky Marmalade (page 27) **and** *Lemon Curd*

BLACKBERRY AND APPLE CURD

Metric/imperial		American
500g/1 lb	cooking apples	1 lb
1kg/2 lb	blackberries	2 lb
	juice of 2 lemons	
250g/8 oz	butter	1 cup
1.25kg/2½ lb	caster sugar	5 cups
	4 eggs	

Peel and core the apples. Wash the blackberries and discard any stems and unripe berries. Cook the apples and berries in very little water until soft.

Pass the pulp through a sieve or purée it in a blender or food processor, then transfer it to a heatproof bowl or the top of a double saucepan (double boiler). Add the lemon juice, butter and sugar to the purée, and heat gently until the butter and sugar have melted.

Beat the eggs well and add them to the mixture. Cook gently over barely simmering water, stirring well, until the mixture thickens.

Pour the curd into small, hot jars, and cover. Alternatively, cool, then pour into small freezer containers, and freeze.

FRESH APRICOT CURD

Metric/imperial		American
250g/8 oz	fresh apricots	8 oz
	grated rind and juice of 1 lemon	
50g/2 oz	butter	¼ cup
250g/8 oz	caster sugar	1 cup
	2 eggs	

Wash the apricots, then cook them in very little water until soft.

Pass the pulp through a sieve or purée it in a blender or food processor, then transfer to a heatproof bowl or the top of a double saucepan (double boiler). Add the rind and juice of the lemon, the butter and sugar to the purée, and heat gently until the butter and sugar have melted.

Beat the eggs well and add them to the mixture. Cook gently over barely simmering water for about 30 minutes, stirring well, until the mixture thickens.

Pour the curd into small, hot jars, and cover. Alternatively, cool, then pour into small freezer containers, and freeze.

GOLDEN CURD

Metric/imperial		American
	2 oranges	
	1 lemon	
50g/2 oz	butter	¼ cup
250g/8 oz	caster sugar	1 cup
	4 eggs	

Grate the orange and lemon rinds finely, squeeze out the juice and strain it.

Melt the butter in a heatproof bowl over barely simmering water or in the top of a double saucepan (double boiler). Add the rind, strained juice and the sugar, and stir until the sugar has dissolved.

Beat the eggs well and add them to the mixture. Cook gently over barely simmering water, stirring well, until the mixture thickens.

Pour the curd into small, hot jars, and cover. Alternatively, cool, then pour into small freezer containers, and freeze.

GOOSEBERRY CURD

Metric/imperial		American
1.5kg/3 lb	green gooseberries	3 lb
375ml/¾ pint	water	2 cups
750g/1½ lb	caster sugar	3 cups
100g/4 oz	butter	½ cup
	4 eggs	

Wash the gooseberries and top and tail them, then cook them in the water until soft.

Pass the pulp through a sieve or purée it in a blender or food processor, then transfer to a heatproof bowl or the top of a double saucepan (double boiler). Add the sugar and butter, and heat gently until they have melted.

Beat the eggs well and add them to the mixture. Cook gently over barely simmering water, stirring well, until the mixture thickens.

Pour the curd into small, hot jars, and cover. Alternatively, cool, then pour into small freezer containers, and freeze.

GOOSEBERRY CHEESE

Metric/imperial		American
1.5kg/3 lb	green gooseberries	3 lb
500ml/1 pint	water	2½ cups
	sugar	

Top and tail the gooseberries and wash them. Simmer them in the water until they are soft.

Pass the pulp through a sieve or purée in a blender or food processor. Weigh or measure the purée and allow 375g/12 oz/¾ US cup sugar to each 500g/1 lb/1 US cup purée. Stir the sugar and purée over low heat until the sugar dissolves. Bring the mixture to the boil, then simmer it gently over low heat, stirring well, until thick.

Test for setting point, then transfer the cheese to small, hot, wide-necked jars, cover and label.

BLACKBERRY CHEESE

Metric/imperial		American
2kg/4 lb	blackberries	4 lb
2 × 5 ml spoons/ 2 teaspoons	citric **or** tartaric acid powder	2 teaspoons
	sugar	

Wash the blackberries and remove any stems and unripe fruit. Put them into a pan with just enough water to cover, then add the acid powder. Bring the mixture to the boil, then simmer gently until the fruit is soft.

Pass the pulp through a sieve or purée it in a blender or food processor, then weigh or measure it. Add the same amount of sugar, and stir over low heat until the sugar dissolves. Bring the purée to the boil, then simmer it gently, stirring well, until thick.

Test for setting point, then transfer the cheese to small, hot, wide-necked jars, cover and label.

SLOE CHEESE

Metric/imperial		American
2kg/4 lb	sloes	4 lb
	sugar	

Wash the fruit, then simmer it in a very little water until it is soft.

Pass the fruit through a sieve or purée it in a blender or food processor, then weigh or measure it. Add the same amount of sugar, and stir over low heat until the sugar dissolves. Bring the mixture to the boil, then simmer gently, stirring well, until thick.

Test for setting point, then transfer the cheese to small, hot, wide-necked jars, cover and label.

Note Sloes make a delicious and slightly sharp fruit cheese.

Blackberry Cheese

Plum and Apple Butter

Metric/imperial		American
1.5kg/3 lb	apples	3 lb
500g/1 lb	plums	1 lb
	sugar	

Peel and core the apples and cut them up. Wash the plums and cut them into pieces, taking out the stones. Mix the fruit, and simmer it in a very little water until soft.

Pass the pulp through a sieve or purée it in a blender or food processor. Weigh or measure the purée and add 375g/12 oz/ ¾ US cup sugar to each 500g/1 lb/1 US cup purée. Stir the sugar into the fruit over low heat until the sugar has dissolved, then boil it until thick and creamy, stirring all the time.

Test for setting point, then transfer the butter to small, hot jars, cover and label.

Cherry Butter

Metric/imperial		American
2kg/4 lb	cherries	4 lb
1kg/2 lb	sugar	2 lb
	grated rind and juice of 1 lemon	

Stone the cherries and crack open a few of the stones. Remove the kernels, blanch them in boiling water, then skin them. Reserve the kernels.

Arrange the cherries in layers with the sugar in a bowl. Add the rind and juice of the lemon, and leave overnight.

Transfer the mixture to a pan, and simmer for 20 minutes, then add the kernels. Boil the mixture quickly until it becomes very thick, stirring all the time.

Test for setting point, then transfer the butter to small, hot jars, cover and label.

Rhubarb Butter

Metric/imperial		American
1kg/2 lb	rhubarb	2 lb
125ml/¼ pint	water	⅔ cup
500g/1 lb	sugar	2 cups
	red food colouring (optional)	

Wash the rhubarb and cut it into pieces. Put into a pan with the water, and simmer until tender.

Pass the rhubarb through a sieve or purée it in a blender or a food processor, then return to the pan. Stir in the sugar over low heat until it dissolves, then boil until the mixture is thick and creamy, stirring occasionally. Add a little red food colouring, if liked, to the pale brown mixture.

Test for setting point, then transfer the butter to small, hot jars, cover and label.

Mincemeat

Fruit mincemeat is a favourite preserve with a long history. It was originally made with minced meat (sometimes tongue) mixed with dried fruit and a lot of spice, together with apples and sugar and a preservative alcoholic spirit. Many of the old ingredients remain, but the meat has been replaced by shredded suet.

The mincemeat looks best if it is composed of a mixture of minced, chopped and whole fruit, and it should be packed into clean, dry, cold jars. A thick covering of brown or greaseproof paper, or a plastic or screw-top will prevent evaporation and drying out, but if the mixture does become a little dry, extra spirits may be stirred in before use. The flavours mature after a week or two, so be sure to make mincemeat well ahead of the time it will be needed.

Basic Fruit Mincemeat

Metric/imperial		American
250g/8 oz	cooking apples	8 oz
250g/8 oz	shredded suet	8 oz
250g/8 oz	raisins	1½ cups
250g/8 oz	currants	1¼ cups
250g/8 oz	sultanas (golden raisins)	1½ cups
100g/4 oz	chopped mixed peel	⅔ cup
	grated rind and juice of 1 lemon	
100g/4 oz	soft brown sugar	½ cup
2 × 15 ml spoons/2 tablespoons	brandy **or** sherry	2 tablespoons

Peel and core the apples. Put them through the coarse screen of a mincer with the suet, dried fruit and mixed peel, or process the mixture in a food processor until fairly finely chopped.

Transfer the mixture to a large bowl. Stir in the rind and juice of the lemon, the sugar and the brandy or sherry, then pack into clean, cold jars. Cover at once, then label.

RICH FRUIT MINCEMEAT

Metric/imperial		American
1kg/2 lb	cooking apples	2 lb
375g/12 oz	shredded suet	3 cups
250g/8 oz	raisins	1½ cups
250g/8 oz	sultanas (golden raisins)	1½ cups
500g/1 lb	currants	2½ cups
250g/8 oz	chopped mixed peel	1⅓ cups
	grated rind and juice of 1 lemon	
15g/½ oz	ground cinnamon	½ tablespoon
750g/1½ lb	soft brown sugar	3 cups
2 × 5 ml spoons/ 2 teaspoons	salt	2 teaspoons
125ml/¼ pint	brandy	⅔ cup
125ml/¼ pint	sherry	⅔ cup

Peel and core the apples. Put them through the coarse screen of a mincer with the suet, dried fruit and mixed peel, or process the mixture in batches in a food processor until fairly finely chopped.

Transfer the mixture to a large bowl. Stir in the rind and juice of the lemon with the cinnamon, sugar, salt, brandy and sherry, and leave the mixture in a cold place for 12 hours.

Stir the mixture well and leave it for another 12 hours.

Pack the mincemeat into clean, cold jars, cover at once, then label.

Note This mincemeat will improve if kept for 6 weeks before use.

CIDER MINCEMEAT

Metric/imperial		American
375g/12 oz	cooking apples	12 oz
375g/12 oz	seedless raisins	2¼ cups
175g/6 oz	currants	1 cup
175g/6 oz	soft brown sugar	¾ cup
2 × 5 ml spoons/ 2 teaspoons	ground cinnamon	2 teaspoons
1 × 5 ml spoon/ 1 teaspoon	ground cloves	1 teaspoon
1 × 5 ml spoon/ 1 teaspoon	ground nutmeg	1 teaspoon
75ml/3 fl oz	dry (hard) cider	⅓ cup
	grated rind and juice of 1 lemon	
75g/3 oz	butter	⅓ cup
1 × 15 ml spoon/ 1 tablespoon	brandy	1 tablespoon

Peel and core the apples. Chop them into small pieces and put into a pan. Add the raisins, currants, sugar, spices, cider, lemon rind and juice and the butter. Simmer the mixture for 30 minutes, stirring well.

Remove the pan from the heat and stir in the brandy. Pack the mincemeat into clean, cold jars, and cover when the mincemeat is cold, then label.

Note This is a short-keeping mincemeat which is best used within 2 weeks, but it can be kept longer in a refrigerator, if necessary.

Rum Mincemeat

Metric/imperial		American
500g/1 lb	cooking apples	1 lb
750g/1½ lb	shredded suet	6 cups
500g/1 lb	currants	2½ cups
500g/1 lb	seedless raisins	3 cups
500g/1 lb	sultanas (golden raisins)	3 cups
500g/1 lb	dark soft brown sugar	2 cups
25g/1 oz	ground mixed spice	2 tablespoons
	grated rind and juice of 2 lemons	
	grated rind and juice of 3 oranges	
125ml/¼ pint	rum	⅔ cup
125ml/¼ pint	brandy	⅔ cup

Peel and core the apples. Put them through the coarse screen of a mincer with the suet, or process in a food processor until fairly finely chopped.

Transfer the apples to a large bowl, and stir in the currants, raisins, sultanas, sugar and spice. Add the rind and juice of the lemons and oranges together with the rum and brandy. Mix together very thoroughly, then pack into clean, cold jars. Cover at once, then label.

Glacé Fruit Mincemeat

Metric/imperial		American
	2 cooking apples	
500g/1 lb	shredded suet	1 lb
500g/1 lb	seedless raisins	3 cups
500g/1 lb	currants	2½ cups
500g/1 lb	sultanas (golden raisins)	3 cups
250g/8 oz	chopped mixed peel	1 cup
100g/4 oz	glacé (candied) cherries, finely chopped	½ cup
50g/2 oz	crystallized (candied) ginger, finely chopped	½ cup
25g/1 oz	glacé (candied) pineapple, finely chopped	2 tablespoons
100g/4 oz	blanched almonds, shredded	1 cup
375g/12 oz	soft brown sugar	1½ cups
1 × 2.5 ml spoon/ ½ teaspoon	ground nutmeg	½ teaspoon
1 × 2.5 ml spoon/ ½ teaspoon	ground mixed spice	½ teaspoon
1 × 2.5 ml spoon/ ½ teaspoon	salt	½ teaspoon
	grated rind and juice of 1 orange	
	grated rind of 1 lemon	
125ml/¼ pint	brandy	⅔ cup

Peel and core the apples. Put them through the coarse screen of a mincer with the suet and raisins.

Transfer the mixture to a large bowl. Stir in the remaining ingredients, and pack into clean, cold jars. Cover, then label.

PICKLES AND CHUTNEYS

Surplus fruit and vegetables can be turned into delicious and useful pickles and chutneys by preserving them in vinegar and sugar with spices. One particular advantage of these spicy relishes is that they can usually be made with a selection of mixed raw materials, so that the odd cauliflower, a few onions, some windfall apples or a spare vegetable marrow or large courgettes (zucchini) need never be wasted, and the resulting preserves will be delicious accompaniments to meat, poultry or fish. As with other kinds of preserve, make a number of varieties in small quantities, rather than an enormous batch of one kind.

Equipment

A large preserving pan or saucepan is necessary to allow room for cooking without boiling over. Stainless steel, aluminium or unchipped enamel are suitable, but iron, brass or copper must never be used as the acid in the preserve will affect the equipment.

Accurate measurements should be used for best results. A large earthenware or ovenproof glass bowl is useful for preparing pickles which need to be brined before cooking. A long-handled wooden spoon should be used exclusively for stirring, and a sharp stainless steel knife is best for speedy cutting.

Some recipes specify the sieving of ingredients, and this should be done through a hair or nylon sieve. This item can also be used for straining spiced vinegar, or the vinegar can be allowed to drip through a jelly bag; a metal strainer should never be used because of the acid content in the preserve. Small pieces of muslin or well-boiled linen are useful for tying up whole spices to add to the pan.

The correct jars must be used for preserves which contain vinegar. They should be clean, sterilized with hot water, then dried and warmed before use. Pickles and chutneys are best stored in wide-mouthed jars. Jam jars with clip-on or screw-top lids, old pickle jars which have been sterilized, all can be used for vinegar-based preserves. Uncoated metal must not touch the finished product, and lids should either be plastic or plastic-coated. Coffee jars with plastic lids are suitable for storage, but paper or transparent jam covers are not suitable as they will allow evaporation. Finally, as with other preserves, labels are essential for identification.

Ingredients

Apart from fruit and/or vegetables, the main ingredients of pickles and chutneys are vinegar, sugar, spices and sometimes salt and dried fruit.

Vinegar should be of good quality and containing at least 5% acetic acid (branded vinegars contain 5–7%). Malt vinegar has a strong flavour and colour, while white vinegar has a better appearance in clear pickles and spiced fruit. Wine vinegar and cider vinegar are more expensive but have a better flavour for more delicate preserves.

Sugar is needed for many pickles and chutneys. Demerara and soft brown sugar are best when a strong colour and flavour are required. Otherwise, granulated or caster sugar can be used.

Pickles

Vegetables and fruit should be of high quality. Blemishes should be removed, and any soft or slushy fruit should be discarded.

Many vegetable pickles are made by brining raw vegetables, draining them and then packing firmly into jars. The jars are then filled with spiced vinegar, sealed tightly and labelled. When a recipe specifies using cooked vegetables, these should be packed into the jars firmly but without pressure which would spoil their shape. The vegetables should stand in the jars for 1 hour, and any liquid should be drained off before the vinegar is poured in.

Fruit is normally lightly cooked in the sweetened spiced vinegar before draining and packing in jars. The vinegar syrup then has to be cooked until syrupy and thickened before being poured over the fruit while hot. Pickles should be stored in a cool, dry dark place.

Pickles are generally ready to eat after about 2 weeks. Some raw vegetable pickles can lose their crispness within a year, and red cabbage is only at its best for 6 months. Spiced pickled fruit is best stored for 2 months before using.

If pickles do not keep well, they have been poorly stored or packed in unclean jars. Under-brining with too little salt can leave too much water in the vegetables which reduces the strength of vinegar and affects its preserving qualities. If pickles ferment, grow mould or show white speckles, they should be thrown away – this may have resulted from weak vinegar, poor brining or bad fruit or vegetables.

BRINING

Raw vegetables for pickling generally need to be brined; this draws out some of their natural liquid which will otherwise dilute the preserving vinegar. Cooked vegetables need not be brined since cooking drives off liquid. Fruit contains natural acid and, therefore, does not need to be brined.

A dry brine or a wet brine can be used. The salt used should be pickling salt, as ordinary salt contains a chemical which keeps it free-running but may cloud the vinegar, and pickling salt is very pure.

To prepare vegetables in a *dry brine*, cut or shred them according to the recipe, then arrange them in layers with salt in a large bowl, allowing 75g/3 oz/¼ us cup salt to 750g/1½ lb prepared vegetables. Salt should be used for the top layer in the bowl, and then a cover of cloth or paper should be arranged on top and the bowl put in a cold place. After 24 hours, there will be a lot of liquid in the bowl which needs draining off. The surplus salt should then be rinsed away under cold running water. The vegetables must be well drained before further processing.

To prepare vegetables in a *wet brine*, put the prepared vegetables into a large bowl and cover them with a salt solution (brine). Allow 250g/8 oz/¾ us cup salt to each 2 litres/4 pints/2½ us quarts water. 500ml/1 pint/2½ us cups of this brine will generally be enough for 500g/1 lb vegetables and should cover them completely. Put a lightly weighted plate on top to keep the vegetables under the brine for the required time. Drain off the liquid completely before further processing.

SPICED VINEGAR

Spiced vinegar is needed for many pickles, and this should be prepared up to a month beforehand so that the vinegar is more fully flavoured with the spices. Ground spices should not be used as they will make the vinegar cloudy.

Allow one 7.5cm/3 inch length cinnamon stick, 15g/½ oz/1 us tablespoon blade mace, 15g/½ oz/3 us tablespoons allspice berries, 8g/¼ oz/1 us tablespoon peppercorns, 8g/¼ oz/1 us tablespoon whole cloves to each 2 litres/4 pints/2½ us quarts vinegar. Crush them lightly with a weight to release their flavour. Tie the spices in a piece of muslin, then put the bag in a pan with the vinegar. Bring the mixture slowly to simmering point, keeping the pan covered so that no flavour is lost. Remove from the heat and leave to stand for about 3 hours before use, or keep in a covered jar in a cold place for a month. Strain and use hot or cold as required.

PICKLING VINEGAR

This is available commercially, and can be used instead of spiced vinegar. Follow the instructions on the bottle.

PICKLED ONIONS

Metric/imperial		American
1kg/2 lb	small pickling **or** pearl onions **or** shallots	2 lb
40g/1½ oz	salt	3 tablespoons
1 litre/2 pints	spiced vinegar (page 55) **or** pickling vinegar	5 cups

Peel the onions or shallots, and put them on a shallow dish. Sprinkle them with salt, cover, then leave overnight.

Drain off the liquid completely, then pack the onions into preserving jars, arranging them with the handle of a wooden spoon so that there are no large spaces. Fill the jars with cold spiced or pickling vinegar, and seal tightly. Leave for 3–4 weeks before using.

PICKLED RED CABBAGE

Metric/imperial		American
1kg/2 lb	red cabbage	2 lb
100g/4 oz	salt	⅓ cup
750ml/1½ pints	spiced vinegar (page 55) **or** pickling vinegar	3¾ cups

Remove the coarse outer leaves and stem from the cabbage. Shred the cabbage finely, then put into a bowl in layers with the salt. Cover, then leave for 24 hours.

Drain off the liquid completely and rinse the cabbage under cold running water. Drain thoroughly, then pack loosely in preserving jars, filling them half-full. Cover with cold vinegar.

Press down the cabbage slightly, and fill the jars up with more cabbage. Cover with more vinegar, then seal tightly. Leave for at least a week before using.

PICKLED BEETROOT

Metric/imperial		American
	8 medium-sized beetroot (beets)	
1 litre/2 pints	vinegar	5 cups
15g/½ oz	black peppercorns	1½ tablespoons
15g/½ oz	allspice berries	3 tablespoons
1 × 5 ml spoon/ 1 teaspoon	grated horseradish	1 teaspoon
1 × 5 ml spoon/ 1 teaspoon	salt	1 teaspoon

Cook the beetroot, then cool, skin and slice them. Pack into preserving jars.

Put the vinegar, spices, horseradish and salt into a pan, bring to the boil, then let the mixture cool. When it is cold, pour the vinegar mixture over the beetroot, and seal the jars at once.

Variations

Beetroot and Onion Pickle
Arrange layers of sliced cooked beetroot and thinly sliced raw onions in jars, and cover them with cold spiced vinegar.

Beetroot and Horseradish Pickle
After cooking the beetroot, grate it and mix with two pieces of grated fresh horseradish and 50g/2 oz/¼ US cup sugar. Pack the mixture into preserving jars, and cover with plain vinegar.

Pickled Onions

56

PICKLED CUCUMBERS

Metric/imperial		American
1kg/2 lb	ridge cucumbers (see **Note**)	2 lb
1 litre/2 pints	wet brine (page 55)	5 cups
50g/2 oz	granulated **or** caster sugar	¼ cup
1 litre/2 pints	spiced vinegar (page 55) **or** pickling vinegar	5 cups
	bay leaves	

Wipe the cucumbers, cut them in half without peeling, then cut them in quarters lengthways. Put them in a large bowl, and cover with the brine. Weight them and leave for 24 hours.

Put the sugar and vinegar into a saucepan, and heat gently until the sugar has dissolved, then cool. Meanwhile, lift the cucumbers out of the brine and rinse them in cold water. Drain them and leave for 2 hours.

Pack the cucumbers upright in preserving jars, and cover them with the cold vinegar syrup. Put a bay leaf in each jar, and seal tightly.

Note Use young cucumbers with soft skins.

PICKLED GHERKINS

Metric/imperial	American
gherkins (pickling cucumbers)	
wet brine (page 55)	
vinegar	
spiced vinegar (page 55) **or** pickling vinegar	

Gather the gherkins on a dry day and wipe them well. Put them in a large bowl, and cover with the brine. Weight them and leave for 3 days.

Drain the gherkins, then cover them with boiling plain vinegar. Leave for 24 hours.

Drain off the vinegar, re-boil it and pour it over the gherkins. Leave for another 24 hours, and repeat the process until the gherkins are bright green.

Drain off the vinegar, pack the gherkins into small jars, and cover them with cold spiced or pickling vinegar. Seal tightly.

PICKLED GREEN TOMATOES

Metric/imperial		American
1kg/2 lb	green tomatoes	2 lb
250g/8 oz	onions	8 oz
100g/4 oz	salt	⅓ cup
250g/8 oz	granulated **or** caster sugar	1 cup
500ml/1 pint	white vinegar	2½ cups

Wipe but do not peel the tomatoes, then cut them across into slices. Peel and slice the onions thinly. Arrange the tomatoes and onions in a bowl in alternate layers, sprinkling the layers generously with the salt. Cover, then leave for 24 hours.

Drain off the liquid completely. Put the sugar and vinegar into a pan, and heat gently over low heat until the sugar has dissolved. Add the tomatoes and onions, and simmer them until soft but not broken. Transfer to warm preserving jars with the simmering liquid, and seal at once.

PICKLED MUSHROOMS

Metric/imperial		American
500g/1 lb	button mushrooms	1 lb
500ml/1 pint	white vinegar	2½ cups
1 × 5 ml spoon/ 1 teaspoon	salt	1 teaspoon
1 × 2.5 ml spoon/½ teaspoon	ground white pepper	½ teaspoon
	a small piece of root (fresh) ginger	
	1 small onion, sliced	

Wipe the mushrooms, but do not wash or peel them, and trim the bottom of their stalks.

Put the mushrooms into a pan with the other ingredients, then simmer the mixture until the mushrooms are tender. Lift out the mushrooms with a slotted spoon, and pack them into preserving jars. Remove the onion and ginger from the vinegar, and bring to the boil. Pour the vinegar over the mushrooms, then seal the jars tightly.

PICKLED APPLES AND PEPPERS

Metric/imperial		American
2kg/4 lb	eating apples	4 lb
1kg/2 lb	green peppers	2 lb
1.5 litres/ 3 pints	cider vinegar	7½ cups
150g/5 oz	soft brown sugar	¾ cup
25g/1 oz	juniper berries	⅓ cup

Peel and core the apples and cut them into rings. De-seed the peppers and cut them into rings. Pack the apples and pepper rings in alternating layers in hot preserving jars.

Bring the vinegar, sugar and juniper berries to the boil, then pour the mixture over the apples and peppers at once, and seal tightly.

PICKLED HORSERADISH

Metric/imperial	American
fresh horseradish roots	
salt	
vinegar	

Wash the roots well in hot water and scrape off the skin. Grate or chop the flesh and pack it into small jars. Use 1 × 5 ml spoon/ 1 teaspoon salt to each 250ml/½ pint/1¼ US cups vinegar, mix well and use to cover the horseradish. Seal the jars tightly.

PICKLED PEACHES

Metric/imperial		American
2kg/4 lb	small ripe peaches	4 lb
1kg/2 lb	granulated **or** caster sugar	4 cups
500ml/1 pint	white vinegar	2½ cups
25g/1 oz	cloves	4 tablespoons
25g/1 oz	allspice berries	6 tablespoons
	2–3 cinnamon sticks	

Wash and wipe the peaches. Put the sugar and vinegar into a pan and dissolve the sugar over gentle heat.

Tie the spices in a piece of muslin, then crush them and put the bag into the pan. Add the peaches, and simmer until they are tender but not soft.

Lift out the peaches with a slotted spoon, and put them into hot preserving jars. Discard the muslin bag, then boil the liquid for 10 minutes or until it becomes syrupy.

Cover the peaches with the vinegar syrup, and seal the jars at once.

PICKLED PLUMS

Metric/imperial		American
1kg/2 lb	plums (see **Note**)	2 lb
	2.5cm/1 inch length cinnamon stick	
1 × 5 ml spoon/ 1 teaspoon	cloves	1 teaspoon
	10 allspice berries	
	1 blade of mace	
500ml/1 pint	white vinegar	2½ cups
750g/1½ lb	granulated **or** caster sugar	3 cups

Wipe the plums and prick each one four times with a needle, then put them into a bowl. Tie the spices in a piece of muslin, then crush them. Put the vinegar and sugar into a pan with the spices, and boil for 10 minutes or until syrupy.

Pour the liquid over the plums and leave overnight.

Drain off the liquid from the plums, and boil it for a further 10 minutes. Pour it back over the fruit, and leave for 12 hours.

Put the plums and liquid into a pan, and bring to the boil. Remove the plums with a slotted spoon, and put them into hot preserving jars. Discard the muslin bag, then boil the liquid again.

Cover the plums with the vinegar syrup, and seal the jars at once.

Note Small black eating plums are best for this recipe.

PICKLED PEARS

Metric/imperial		American
2kg/4 lb	cooking pears	4 lb
1kg/2 lb	granulated **or** caster sugar	4 cups
500ml/1 pint	white vinegar	2½ cups
25g/1 oz	cloves	4 tablespoons
25g/1 oz	allspice berries	6 tablespoons
25g/1 oz	root (fresh) ginger	1 oz
	2–3 cinnamon sticks	
	rind of ½ lemon	

Peel and core the pears and cut them into quarters. Put the sugar and vinegar into a pan, and dissolve the sugar over gentle heat.

Tie the spices and lemon rind in a piece of muslin, then crush them and put the bag into the pan. Put in the pear quarters, and simmer until tender but not broken.

Lift out the pears with a slotted spoon, then transfer them to hot preserving jars. Discard the muslin bag, and boil the liquid for 10 minutes or until it becomes syrupy.

Cover the fruit with the syrup, and seal the jars tightly.

PICKLED DATES

Metric/imperial		American
1kg/2 lb	succulent dessert dates	2 lb
	white vinegar	
	12 peppercorns	
	10 cloves	
	a small piece of cinnamon stick	
1 × 5ml spoon/ 1 teaspoon	salt	1 teaspoon

Stone the dates and put them into preserving jars. Measure out the amount of vinegar required to cover the dates, and allow the given quantities of spices and salt to each 500ml/1 pint/ 2½ US cups vinegar needed.

Tie the spices in a piece of muslin, crush them and put the bag into a pan. Add the measured vinegar, and bring to the boil. Discard the muslin and pour the hot vinegar over the dates, then seal the jars tightly. Leave the dates for 1 month before using them.

PICKLED EGGS

Metric/imperial		American
1 litre/2 pints	white vinegar	5 cups
15g/½ oz	root (fresh) ginger	½ oz
15g/½ oz	mustard seeds	1 tablespoon
15g/½ oz	white peppercorns	1½ tablespoons
	12 hard-boiled eggs	
	2 small chillies, fresh **or** dried	

Simmer the vinegar for 5 minutes with the ginger, bruised, the mustard seeds and peppercorns, then strain and leave the vinegar to cool.

Shell the cooled eggs. Arrange them upright in one or more wide-mouthed preserving jars, and put the chillies on top. Cover with the vinegar, and seal the jars tightly. Leave for 2–3 weeks before serving.

PICKLED WALNUTS

Metric/imperial		American
	green walnuts (see **Note**)	
2 litres/4 pints	wet brine (page 55)	2½ quarts
2 litres/4 pints	vinegar	2½ quarts
	3 small onions	
1 × 5ml spoon/ 1 teaspoon	cloves	1 teaspoon
40g/1½ oz	black peppercorns	3½ tablespoons
25g/1 oz	root (fresh) ginger	1 oz
	2 blades mace	
	2 bay leaves	
50g/2 oz	mustard seeds	4 tablespoons

Piece each nut with a darning needle, and put into a large bowl. Cover with brine. Weight the nuts, and leave for 9 days, changing the brine every 3 days.

Drain the walnuts, and put on flat dishes, then leave in an airy place for 2–3 days until the nuts are black.

Put the vinegar, onions and spices into a saucepan, and boil for 5 minutes. Leave, covered, for 2 hours, then strain and boil again.

Pack the walnuts into preserving jars, and cover with the hot vinegar. Leave until cold, then seal tightly. Leave for 2 months before using.

Note Use the walnuts before any shell has formed.

Handling the nuts can stain your hands badly.

MUSTARD PICKLE

Metric/imperial		American
	3–4 large courgettes (zucchini)	
	1 medium-sized cauliflower	
	1 cucumber	
500g/1 lb	French (snap) beans	1 lb
500g/1 lb	pickling onions	1 lb
25g/1 oz	salt	2 tablespoons
1 litre/2 pints	vinegar	5 cups
300g/10 oz	granulated **or** caster sugar	1¼ cups
50g/2 oz	flour	½ cup
50g/2 oz	dry mustard	6 tablespoons
15g/½ oz	turmeric	1 tablespoon
15g/½ oz	ground ginger	1 tablespoon
15g/½ oz	ground nutmeg	1 tablespoon

Chop the courgettes into chunks without peeling them. Divide the cauliflower into small pieces, chop the cucumber and beans, and peel the onions. Mix together the vegetables in a bowl, and sprinkle with the salt. Cover with water, and leave to soak overnight.

Drain off and discard the water from the vegetables. Put the vegetables into a pan with most of the vinegar, and simmer until just tender. Mix all the dry ingredients with the remaining vinegar to a smooth paste.

Add a little of the simmering vinegar to the spicy paste, then mix the paste into the vegetables. Simmer the vegetables for a further 10 minutes, stirring all the time, until thick. Put the pickle into preserving jars while hot, and seal tightly.

CLEAR MIXED PICKLES

Metric/imperial		American
500g/1 lb	shallots	1 lb
500g/1 lb	cauliflower	1 lb
	1 large cucumber	
25g/1 oz	salt	2 tablespoons
1.5 litres/ 3 pints	spiced vinegar (page 55) **or** pickling vinegar	7½ cups
15g/½ oz	pickling spice	3 tablespoons

Peel the shallots. Divide the cauliflower into florets. Peel the cucumber, and cut into cubes. Mix all the vegetables in a bowl, sprinkle with the salt, cover, then leave overnight.

Drain off the liquid completely, and pack the vegetables into preserving jars. Pour over the cold vinegar, and divide the pickling spice among the jars. Seal tightly and leave the pickle for a few months before using it.

Mustard Pickle

SPICED APPLE SLICES

Metric/imperial		American
1.5kg/3 lb	eating apples	3 lb
500g/1 lb	granulated **or** caster sugar	2 cups
500ml/1 pint	white vinegar	2½ cups
1 × 5ml spoon/ 1 teaspoon	salt	1 teaspoon
125ml/¼ pint	water	⅔ cup
	1 cinnamon stick	
2 × 5ml spoons/ 2 teaspoons	cloves	2 teaspoons

Peel and core the apples and slice them thickly. Put the sugar, vinegar, salt and water into a pan, and dissolve the sugar over gentle heat.

Tie the spices in a piece of muslin, then crush them and put the bag into the pan. Put in the apple slices, and simmer until tender but not broken.

Lift out the apple slices with a slotted spoon, and put them into hot preserving jars. Discard the muslin bag, then boil the liquid until syrupy.

Cover the apples with the hot liquid, and seal the jars tightly.

SPICED APRICOTS

Metric/imperial		American
500g/1 lb	dried apricots	1 lb
15g/½ oz	cloves	2 tablespoons
	a small piece of cinnamon stick	
15g/½ oz	allspice berries	3 tablespoons
750ml/1½ pints	white vinegar	3¾ cups
600g/1¼ lb	granulated **or** caster sugar	2½ cups

Put the apricots in a bowl, cover them with water and leave to soak overnight.

Tie the spices in a piece of muslin, crush them and put the bag into a pan. Add the vinegar, and bring to the boil. Drain the apricots, then add them to the vinegar and simmer for 10 minutes.

Lift out the apricots with a slotted spoon, and transfer them to hot preserving jars. Stir the sugar into the vinegar, bring the mixture to the boil, and boil for 5 minutes or until the mixture becomes syrupy.

Discard the bag of spices, pour the syrup over the fruit, and seal the jars tightly.

Spiced Cranberries

Metric/imperial		American
2kg/4 lb	cranberries	4 lb
375ml/¾ pint	cider vinegar	2 cups
125ml/¼ pint	water	⅔ cup
1.5kg/3 lb	granulated **or** caster sugar	6 cups
25g/1 oz	ground cinnamon	1 tablespoon
15g/½ oz	ground cloves	1 tablespoon
15g/½ oz	ground allspice	1 tablespoon

Put all the ingredients into a pan, bring the mixture to the boil, then simmer it for 45 minutes, stirring well.

Pour the mixture into hot preserving jars, and seal them tightly.

Spiced Melon

Metric/imperial		American
2.5kg/5 lb	melon (see **Note**)	5 lb
50g/2 oz	salt	4 tablespoons
500ml/1 pint	water	2½ cups
500g/1 lb	granulated **or** caster sugar	2 cups
500ml/1 pint	white vinegar	2½ cups
	8 cloves	
	a small piece of cinnamon stick	

Peel the melon and cut the flesh into 2.5cm/1 inch dice, then weigh or measure the prepared flesh. Put 2kg/4 lb/6½ US cups into a bowl, and cover with the salt and water. Leave overnight.

Drain off the brine, put the melon in a pan and cover with cold water. Bring the mixture to the boil, and simmer until the melon is transparent and tender but not broken. Meanwhile, boil together the sugar, vinegar and spices in another pan for 20 minutes.

Strain the sugar mixture and bring it back to the boil. Drain the melon and add it to the sugar mixture. Continue to boil for 10 minutes, then pour it into hot preserving jars, and seal tightly.

Note Small sweet melons are most suitable. Do not use watermelon.

SPICED ORANGES

Metric/imperial		American
	6 thin-skinned oranges	
2½ × 5ml spoons/2½ teaspoons	cloves	2½ teaspoons
	7.5cm/3 inch length cinnamon stick	
375ml/¾ pint	white vinegar	2 cups
375g/12 oz	granulated **or** caster sugar	1½ cups

Wipe the oranges and slice them across into thin rounds. Do not peel them. Put the slices into a pan with enough water to cover, then simmer for 45 minutes or until the rind is tender.

Drain the fruit and discard the cooking liquid. Tie the spices in a piece of muslin, reserving 1–2 cloves, then crush the spices. Put the vinegar and sugar into a pan with the spices, and bring to the boil. Reduce the mixture to simmering point, then add the orange rings, a few at a time. Cook them gently until the rind becomes transparent.

Lift out the fruit with a slotted spoon, and transfer to hot preserving jars. Discard the muslin bag, and boil the liquid for 5 minutes or until it becomes syrupy.

Cover the fruit with the hot liquid, and put the reserved cloves into each jar. Seal them at once.

Chutney

Chutney is a mixture of fruit and/or vegetables cut into small pieces (or minced), then cooked with vinegar, sugar and spices to make a spicy product with the consistency of jam. Fruit and vegetables may be bruised and imperfect, but should never be mouldy or rotten, and all bruises and poor parts should be cut away. Dried fruit, onions, garlic and brown sugar all give added flavour and richness to chutney.

Spices are particularly important in chutney, and may be varied according to family tastes. Cayenne pepper and chillies are very hot and may be omitted from recipes, but ginger which also gives 'hotness' is always acceptable in chutney. Cloves, cinnamon, nutmeg and mace are aromatic spices, and are particularly good for mild fruit chutneys. Use freshly ground spices, and measure them accurately for the first batch of chutney, but vary quantities, if liked, after testing the finished product when cold.

The cooking softens the ingredients, breaks down fibres and brings out flavours. It is continued slowly until the mixture is of a thick jam-like consistency. Chutney will thicken slightly when cool but should never be bottled while pale and liquid. Stir the chutney carefully to prevent sticking, and never cook it, unwatched, for long periods, as it will ruin if burned.

Put the chutney into hot, clean jars with vinegar-proof lids. Never leave them open or cover them with paper as the mixture will dry out. Fill the jars to the brim, and wipe them well before sealing, labelling and storing in a cool, dry, dark place. Chutney matures in storage and is best left for a month or two to develop a good flavour.

If the chutney becomes dry and brown on top, it has been kept without an airtight cover, or the storage place has been too warm. Chutney should be thrown away if it ferments or becomes mouldy. This can result from undercooking with too much water in the mixture, or from unclean jars or covers.

APPLE CHUTNEY

Metric/imperial		American
2.5kg/5 lb	apples	5 lb
500ml/1 pint	vinegar	2½ cups
500g/1 lb	Demerara sugar (or light brown sugar)	2 cups
1 × 5ml spoon/ 1 teaspoon	salt	1 teaspoon
1 × 15ml spoon/ 1 tablespoon	ground ginger	1 tablespoon
	3–6 small chillies, fresh **or** dried (optional)	
250g/8 oz	onions	8 oz
250g/8 oz	stoned dates	8 oz
250g/8 oz	sultanas (golden raisins)	1½ cups

Peel, core and chop the apples. Put the vinegar into a pan with the sugar, salt, ginger and chopped chillies, and bring to the boil. Add the apples, chopped onions, dates and sultanas, and simmer for at least 1 hour or until the mixture is golden-brown and thick. (The apples make a lot of juice and the chutney should not be runny.)

Put the chutney into hot jars, cover and seal them.

AUTUMN CHUTNEY

Metric/imperial		American
2kg/4 lb	apples	4 lb
1kg/2 lb	firm pears	2 lb
1.5kg/3 lb	red tomatoes	3 lb
2kg/4 lb	soft brown sugar	8 cups
250g/8 oz	sultanas (golden raisins)	1½ cups
250g/8 oz	seedless raisins	1½ cups
1 litre/2 pints	vinegar	5 cups
1 × 5ml spoon/ 1 teaspoon	ground mace	1 teaspoon
1 × 5ml spoon/ 1 teaspoon	Cayenne pepper	1 teaspoon
1 × 5ml spoon/ 1 teaspoon	ground cloves	1 teaspoon
1 × 5ml spoon/ 1 teaspoon	pepper	1 teaspoon
2 × 15ml spoons/ 2 tablespoons	salt	2 tablespoons
1 × 5ml spoon/ 1 teaspoon	ground ginger	1 teaspoon

Peel, core and chop the apples and pears. Blanch, skin and chop the tomatoes. Put all the ingredients into a pan, and stir well. Simmer the mixture for 2 hours or until it is golden-brown and thick.

Put the chutney into hot jars, cover and seal them.

APRICOT AND ORANGE CHUTNEY

Metric/imperial		American
500g/1 lb	dried apricots	1 lb
250g/8 oz	granulated sugar	1 cup
100g/4 oz	sultanas (golden raisins)	1 cup
	1 clove of garlic, chopped	
	3 peppercorns	
	grated rind and juice of 1 orange	
250ml/½ pint	white vinegar	1¼ cups

Put the apricots into a bowl, just cover with water, and leave overnight.

Drain off the liquid and put the apricots into a pan with the sugar, sultanas, chopped garlic clove, peppercorns, grated orange rind and juice. Bring the mixture to the boil. Stir in the vinegar, and simmer for 45 minutes or until golden-brown and thick.

Put the chutney into hot jars, cover and seal them.

DRIED APRICOT CHUTNEY

Metric/imperial		American
500g/1 lb	dried apricots	1 lb
750g/1½ lb	onions	1½ lb
500g/1 lb	sugar	2 cups
	grated rind and juice of 2 oranges	
250g/8 oz	sultanas (golden raisins)	1½ cups
750ml/1½ pints	cider vinegar	3¾ cups
2 × 5ml spoons/ 2 teaspoons	salt	2 teaspoons
	2 cloves garlic, crushed	
1 × 5ml spoon/ 1 teaspoon	dry mustard	1 teaspoon
1 × 2.5ml spoon/ ½ teaspoon	ground allspice	½ teaspoon

Put the apricots into a bowl and cover with water. Leave to soak overnight.

Drain the apricots and chop them finely. Put them into a pan with the onions, chopped, the sugar and the grated rind and juice of the oranges. Add the sultanas, vinegar, salt, crushed garlic, mustard and allspice, and simmer the mixture gently for 1 hour until it is golden-brown and thick.

Put the chutney into hot jars, cover and seal them.

BANANA CHUTNEY

Metric/imperial		American
1kg/2 lb	ripe bananas	2 lb
250g/8 oz	stoned dates	8 oz
	grated rind and juice of 1 lemon	
375ml/¾ pint	vinegar	2 cups
250g/8 oz	seedless raisins	1½ cups
250g/8 oz	Demerara sugar (or light brown sugar)	1 cup
250ml/½ pint	syrup from any canned fruit	1¼ cups
100g/4 oz	crystallized ginger, chopped	½ cup
2 × 5ml spoons/ 2 teaspoons	salt	2 teaspoons
4 × 5ml spoons/ 4 teaspoons	curry powder	4 teaspoons

Peel the bananas and cut them into small pieces. Chop the dates and put them into a pan with the bananas. Add the grated rind and juice of the lemon with the vinegar. Cover the pan and cook gently for 1½ hours.

Stir the raisins, sugar, fruit syrup, crystallized ginger, salt and curry powder into the pan. Simmer the mixture for 30 minutes or until golden-brown and thick.

Put the chutney into hot jars, cover and seal them.

BLACKBERRY CHUTNEY

Metric/imperial		American
3kg/6 lb	blackberries	6 lb
1kg/2 lb	cooking apples	2 lb
1kg/2 lb	onions	2 lb
1kg/2 lb	soft brown sugar	2 lb
1 litre/2 pints	vinegar	5 cups
25g/1 oz	salt	2 tablespoons
50g/2 oz	dry mustard	6 tablespoons
50g/2 oz	ground ginger	4 tablespoons
2 × 5ml spoons/ 2 teaspoons	ground mace	2 teaspoons
1 × 5ml spoon/ 1 teaspoon	Cayenne pepper	1 teaspoon

Wash the blackberries, remove the stems and hard berries, and put the rest into a pan. Peel, core and chop the apples and chop the onions. Add the apples and onions to the blackberries with the sugar, vinegar, salt and spices. Simmer for 1½ hours or until golden-brown and thick.

Put the chutney into hot jars, cover and seal them.

FRESH FIG CHUTNEY

Metric/imperial		American
1kg/2 lb	green figs	2 lb
500g/1 lb	onions	1 lb
100g/4 oz	crystallized ginger	4 oz
500ml/1 pint	vinegar	2½ cups
250g/8 oz	soft brown sugar	1 cup
2 × 5ml spoons/ 2 teaspoons	salt	2 teaspoons
1 × 2.5ml spoon/ ½ teaspoon	pepper	½ teaspoon

Wash the figs and cut them into small pieces. Chop the onions and cut the crystallized ginger into pieces the same size as the figs.

Heat the vinegar, sugar, salt and pepper, stirring, until the sugar has dissolved. Add the figs, onions and ginger, and bring the mixture to the boil. Simmer for 45 minutes or until it is golden-brown and thick.

Put the chutney into hot jars, cover and seal them.

DAMSON CHUTNEY

Metric/imperial		American
1.5kg/3 lb	damsons	3 lb
500g/1 lb	apples	1 lb
250g/8 oz	onions	8 oz
250g/8 oz	stoned dates	8 oz
250g/8 oz	soft brown sugar	1 cup
500ml/1 pint	vinegar	2½ cups
15g/½ oz	ground ginger	1 tablespoon
15g/½ oz	dry mustard	1½ tablespoons
15g/½ oz	salt	1 tablespoon
1 × 2.5ml spoon/ ½ teaspoon	pepper	½ teaspoon
1 × 2.5ml spoon/ ½ teaspoon	ground cloves	½ teaspoon

Put the damsons into a pan over low heat, and simmer them in their own juice, removing the stones as they rise to the surface.

Peel, core and chop the apples and chop the onions. Put all the ingredients into a pan, and simmer for 2 hours until soft and thick.

Put the chutney into hot jars, cover and seal them.

PINEAPPLE CHUTNEY

Metric/imperial		American
	1 medium-sized pineapple	
250g/8 oz	sugar	1 cup
125ml/¼ pint	cider vinegar	⅔ cup
1 × 5ml spoon/ 1 teaspoon	ground cloves	1 teaspoon
1 × 5ml spoon/ 1 teaspoon	ground cinnamon	1 teaspoon
1 × 5ml spoon/ 1 teaspoon	ground ginger	1 teaspoon
1 × 15ml spoon/ 1 tablespoon	curry powder	1 tablespoon

Peel and core the pineapple and cut the flesh into small pieces. Put any pineapple juice with the sugar and vinegar into a pan, and bring to the boil. Add the spices, and simmer for 5 minutes.

Add the pineapple flesh, and simmer for 10 minutes, stirring well.

Put the chutney into hot jars, cover and seal them.

Note This chutney has a dominant pineapple texture.

GOOSEBERRY CHUTNEY

Metric/imperial		American
2kg/4 lb	green gooseberries	4 lb
500g/1 lb	soft brown sugar	2 cups
1 litre/2 pints	vinegar	5 cups
500g/1 lb	onions	1 lb
750g/1½ lb	seedless raisins	4½ cups
100g/4 oz	mustard seeds	8 tablespoons
50g/2 oz	ground allspice	3 tablespoons
100g/4 oz	salt	⅓ cup

Top and tail the gooseberries. Mix the sugar with half the vinegar, and boil until a syrup forms.

Add the chopped onions, the raisins, bruised mustard seeds, allspice and salt. Boil the gooseberries in the remaining vinegar until tender.

Put the two mixtures together, and simmer for 1 hour or until golden-brown and thick.

Put the chutney into hot jars, cover and seal them.

ORANGE CHUTNEY

Metric/imperial		American
	6 thin-skinned oranges	
250g/8 oz	onions	8 oz
500g/1 lb	stoned dates	1 lb
500g/1 lb	soft brown sugar	2 cups
500ml/1 pint	vinegar	2½ cups
2 × 5ml spoons/ 2 teaspoons	ground ginger	2 teaspoons
2 × 5ml spoons/ 2 teaspoons	salt	2 teaspoons

Peel the oranges and discard the pips. Chop the flesh and put into a pan with any orange juice, the chopped onions and chopped dates. Add the sugar, vinegar, ginger and salt, and stir well. Simmer the mixture for 1 hour or until golden-brown and thick.

Put the chutney into hot jars, cover and seal them.

PLUM CHUTNEY

Metric/imperial		American
1.5kg/3 lb	plums (see **Note**)	3 lb
500g/1 lb	carrots	1 lb
	6–8 cloves garlic	
	4–6 small chillies, fresh **or** dried (optional)	
500ml/1 pint	vinegar	2½ cups
500g/1 lb	seedless raisins	3 cups
500g/1 lb	soft brown sugar	2 cups
25g/1 oz	ground ginger	2 tablespoons

Cut up the plums and discard the stones. Grate the carrots and chop the garlic and chillies, if used. Put the plums, carrots and vinegar into a pan, and simmer until soft.

Add the remaining ingredients together with the garlic and chillies, and simmer for 1 hour or until golden-brown and thick.

Put the chutney into hot jars, cover and seal them.

Note A mixture of different plums can be used for this chutney.

RHUBARB CHUTNEY

Metric/imperial		American
1kg/2 lb	rhubarb	2 lb
250g/8 oz	onions	8 oz
750g/1½ lb	soft brown sugar	3 cups
250g/8 oz	sultanas (golden raisins)	1½ cups
500ml/1 pint	vinegar	2½ cups
15g/½ oz	dry mustard	1½ tablespoons
1 × 5ml spoon/ 1 teaspoon	ground mixed spice	1 teaspoon
1 × 5ml spoon/ 1 teaspoon	pepper	1 teaspoon
1 × 5ml spoon/ 1 teaspoon	ground ginger	1 teaspoon
1 × 5ml spoon/ 1 teaspoon	salt	1 teaspoon
	a pinch of Cayenne pepper	

Wipe the rhubarb and cut into chunks. Chop the onions. Put all the ingredients into a pan, and stir well. Simmer the mixture for 1 hour or until it is golden-brown and thick.

Put the chutney into hot jars, cover and seal them.

CHERRY CHUTNEY

Metric/imperial		American
1.5kg/3 lb	eating cherries	3 lb
250g/8 oz	seedless raisins	1½ cups
100g/4 oz	soft brown sugar	½ cup
50g/2 oz	runny honey	¼ cup
250ml/½ pint	vinegar	1¼ cups
2 × 5ml spoons/ 2 teaspoons	ground mixed spice	2 teaspoons

Stone the cherries and chop them. Put all the ingredients into a pan, heat them gently and stir until the sugar has dissolved. Bring the mixture to the boil and boil for 5 minutes, then simmer for 30 minutes or until the mixture is golden-brown and thick.

Put the chutney into hot jars, cover and seal them.

Rhubarb Chutney

BEETROOT CHUTNEY

Metric/imperial		American
1kg/2 lb	cooked beetroot (beets)	2 lb
	2 medium-sized onions	
500g/1 lb	apples	1 lb
250g/8 oz	sugar	1 cup
500ml/1 pint	vinegar	2½ cups
1 × 15ml spoon/ 1 tablespoon	lemon juice	1 tablespoon
1 × 2.5ml spoon/ ½ teaspoon	ground ginger	½ teaspoon
1 × 2.5ml spoon/ ½ teaspoon	salt	½ teaspoon

Peel the beetroot, if necessary, and cut it into small cubes. Chop the onions and core and chop the apples. Mix all the ingredients except the beetroot, and bring them to the boil. Simmer for 30 minutes, then add the beetroot, and simmer for a further 15 minutes or until golden-brown and thick.

Put the chutney into hot jars, cover and seal them.

GREEN TOMATO CHUTNEY

Metric/imperial		American
2.5kg/5 lb	green tomatoes	5 lb
500g/1 lb	onions	1 lb
15g/½ oz	pepper	1 tablespoon
25g/1 oz	salt	2 tablespoons
500g/1 lb	soft brown sugar	2 cups
500ml/1 pint	vinegar	2½ cups
250g/8 oz	seedless raisins	1½ cups
250g/8 oz	sultanas (golden raisins)	1½ cups

Slice the tomatoes and chop the onions. Put them into a bowl with the pepper and salt. Mix well and leave the mixture to stand overnight.

Put the sugar and vinegar into a pan and bring to the boil, then add the raisins and sultanas, and bring back to the boil. Simmer for 5 minutes.

Add the tomatoes and onions, and simmer for a further hour or until the mixture is golden-brown and thick.

Put the chutney into hot jars, cover and seal them.

UNCOOKED MINT CHUTNEY

Metric/imperial		American
375ml/¾ pint	cider vinegar	2 cups
500g/1 lb	sugar	2 cups
2 × 5ml spoons/ 2 teaspoons	dry mustard	2 teaspoons
500g/1 lb	eating apples	1 lb
	2 medium-sized onions	
250g/8 oz	fresh mint leaves	8 oz
75g/3 oz	seedless raisins	⅔ cup
	a pinch of salt	

Heat the vinegar in a pan, then stir in the sugar and mustard until the sugar has dissolved. Stir well, remove from the heat and cool slightly.

Chop the apples, onions and mint very finely, and put them in a bowl with the raisins and salt. Pour over the vinegar mixture, mix well, then pour the chutney into hot jars and seal them at once.

RED TOMATO CHUTNEY

Metric/imperial		American
500g/1 lb	red tomatoes	1 lb
100g/4 oz	apples	4 oz
250g/8 oz	onions	8 oz
500g/1 lb	seedless raisins	3 cups
100g/4 oz	soft brown sugar	½ cup
250ml/½ pint	vinegar	1¼ cups
2 × 5ml spoons/ 2 teaspoons	salt	2 teaspoons
2 × 5ml spoons/ 2 teaspoons	ground ginger	2 teaspoons
	a pinch of Cayenne pepper	

Blanch and skin the tomatoes, then chop them. Peel, core and chop the apples and chop the onions. Put all the ingredients into a pan, stir well and simmer for 1 hour or until the mixture is golden-brown and thick.

Put the chutney into hot jars, cover and seal them.

INDEX OF RECIPES